What works for troubled children?

Ann Buchanan and Charlotte Ritchie

Published by Barnardo's
Tanners Lane
Barkingside
Ilford
Essex
IG6 1QG

Charity registration no 216250

First published 1999
Second edition 2004

Designed and produced by Andrew Haig & Associates

Printed in the United Kingdom by Russell Press, Nottingham

A catalogue record for this book is available from the British Library

ISBN 1 904659 03 9

Contents

B.C.F.T.C.S.

vii

Figures and tables

Figures

Tables

About the authors

Dr Ann Buchanan is Director of the Centre for Research into Parenting and Children and Reader in Social Work at the University of Oxford.

Dr Charlotte Ritchie is a research associate at the Centre for Research into Parenting and Children.

Foreword

It is a challenging paradox of the times we live in that while children's physical health and living conditions have substantially improved in developed countries over the last half century, their overall mental health has apparently deteriorated. Worrying increases have been noted in a range of specific disorders, for example, depression, conduct and eating disorders, suicidal behaviours and substance misuse (Rutter and Smith, 1995). Children are less likely to die young or suffer disabling illnesses and, as adults, they will live longer. However, the strains and stresses in children's lives are taking their toll to such an extent that the overall issue of their emotional well-being can be seen as one of the most important public health issues facing us today.

A substantial minority of children – up to 45 per cent – are likely to have moderate or severe psychological problems at some time in childhood or early adulthood. A large proportion of these children recover without the need for any specialist help. Many children, of course, will experience only transitory problems. Previous work by Dr Buchanan has illustrated how half of those children having problems at any given age had no such problems a few years later (Buchanan and Ten Brinke, 1998). However, at any one time it is suggested that up to 20 per cent of children and young people may be affected by emotional and behavioural problems, mostly anxiety disorders, disruptive disorders and Attention Deficit Hyperactivity Disorder (ADHD) (Mental Health Foundation, 1999). These difficulties are not distributed evenly throughout the population: poverty, poor housing and poor educational attainment are associated with higher levels of prevalence. While we should never underestimate children's capacity for recovery, a worrying continuity has been observed between childhood problems and adult outcomes, particularly where no effective interventions have been offered to children and their parents at the point at which the difficulties emerge.

The first edition of this volume in Barnardo's 'What works?' series resulted from a collaboration between Barnardo's and a local authority. This book differed from others in the series in that it comprised an exhaustive review of research combined with the experience of social care practitioners from Wiltshire. Rather than review the evidence for effective interventions and convey the results to practitioners, the generation of the book began with a detailed consultation exercise to identify the types of problems – and the solutions offered – that were part of the working lives of social care practitioners. The result was a book that summarised the most robust knowledge we had of how children could be helped, while remaining rooted in the day-to-day reality of the people affected – practitioners, children and families. The publication of a second edition is a reflection of the continuing importance of this issue. While arising primarily from consultation with social workers, we believe this report has relevance for anyone providing help to children and families within the health and social care field.

Barnardo's and Wiltshire County Council Department for Children and Education (formerly social services) have developed an excellent working relationship over the past decade, both in the development of innovative services and the joint commissioning of research, and most recently through Wiltshire's 'Pathways' project (www.WiltshirePathways.org). This book is a further example of how the respective strengths of the statutory, voluntary and academic sectors can combine to produce results of a quality that none could have achieved alone.

Chris Hanvey, UK Director Children's Services, Barnardo's

Bob Wolfson, Director for Children and Education, Wiltshire County Council

Acknowledgements

When the original edition of *What works for troubled children?* was published in 1999 we were surprised at the demand: it seemed to fill a yawning gap. Now, five years later, there is more information available on 'what works'. It therefore makes sense, in this new edition, to incorporate some of what is new.

The starting point for the original book was some 40 or more anonymised case vignettes sent in by experienced social workers who were supporting families in Wiltshire. In half of these cases the social workers felt their intervention had been 'successful' and in the other half they felt they had been 'unsuccessful'. These vignettes briefly outlined the case; the type of problem; the type of need that as social workers they had tried to meet; the services and therapies provided; and the reasons why they thought their intervention had been 'successful' or 'unsuccessful'.

The case studies vividly described the kinds of issues that front-line family support workers struggle with daily, and their enormous skill and ingenuity in helping families cope with a wide array of problems in what might have appeared to be intractable situations.

We all met at a workshop on 18 June 1998 and discussed:

- how we should categorise different types of need
- the understanding we had gained from practice about what works best in what type of situation.

Our remit thereafter was to undertake a review of research and report on the evidence base for effective interventions. It quickly became apparent that in one way or another most cases involved 'troubled children' and that a central component in supporting families was responding to children with emotional and behavioural problems. This, then, became the focus of the book.

We would, again, like to thank these Wiltshire social workers for reminding us of the front-line issues and for playing such an important part in this book. We also owe a debt of thanks to the staff who spent time critically reading the first draft.

In addition, we owe a special debt of thanks to Peter Fanshawe from Wiltshire

Children and Families Branch and Tony Newman from Barnardo's Research and Development Section for initiating this project.

Ann Buchanan and Charlotte Ritchie, Oxford 2003

Extracts from case vignettes

'Father physically and emotionally violent and aggressive to wife and children … children all lack self-esteem.'

'Thirteen-year-old, previously abused in care, constantly running away from home and missing school.'

'Three-year-old boy has severe behavioural difficulties that seem to be worse with his mother. Mother depressed.'

'Mother's ill health often meant that she could not cope with parenting the three young children. One child under treatment for Attention Deficit Hyperactivity Disorder (ADHD).'

'Fifteen-year-old with minor disability suffered severe bullying at school. Now very withdrawn.'

'Following domestic violence mother and three young children lived in a refuge. Mother and children severely traumatised by experiences. School concerned about the children's progress.'

'Oldest boy over-chastised … now copying behaviour of father with young siblings.'

'Fifteen-year-old girl becoming out of control at home. She is verbally and physically assaulting mother.'

'Mother with learning disabilities and father with mental health problems. Eldest child under pressure and distressed, second child age 11 drinking and staying out late.'

'Mrs X refused to have son home when he was excluded from residential school because of his difficult behaviour.'

'XY referred to us two years ago when his foster placement broke down due to difficult behaviour.'

'Lone parent at end of tether; could harm the children. Can't get children age 6 and 7 to bed at nights.'

Extracts from case vignettes given by practising social workers in Wiltshire. Identifying details have been changed to preserve anonymity.

Introduction

> Though troubled children and teenagers are common, many of them have social or educational problems rather than health problems. These require social and educational solutions, not health interventions. (Goodman, 1997a, pp4–5)

This book is not intended to turn family support workers, social workers, teachers and other front-line workers into psychologists or psychiatrists. Children with severe emotional and behaviour disorders need the help of mental health services. The purpose of this book is to outline 'evidence-based' social and educational strategies that may be helpful for the many children and young people who have less serious emotional and behavioural difficulties. Although offending behaviour can be an end product of such difficulties, these behaviours are not a primary focus of this book. Similarly, strategies for managing challenging behaviour in people with learning disabilities are not included.

This book is aimed at professionals offering Tier One and in some cases Tier Two mental health services as defined by the Health Advisory Service (1995):

> Tier One consists of professionals such as GPs, social workers, voluntary sector workers, school staff, police officers, school medical officers, school nurses, health visitors who are not necessarily employed for the prime purpose of promoting mental health, but who directly and indirectly influence the mental health of children through their work with them. They are usually the first point of contact between a child or family and the child care or health agencies.

This book may also be useful to Tier Two workers:

> Tier Two in the social and education services, may be represented by specifically tasked social workers, pupil support teachers, or educational psychologists.

Further information on the tier system is given in Chapter 5.

'Troubled behaviour' in children and young people may relate directly to the adversities besetting their families that social workers and other front-line professionals are trying to alleviate. Children's behaviour may improve once the stresses are lifted.

1

Some 'troubled behaviour' seen in the children and young people may be a direct communication of the distress they are experiencing. It is important to hear the message. Their behaviour may improve when the message is heard and appropriate action taken.

Sometimes, however, the emotional and behavioural difficulties remain long after the original message of distress, and get in the way of progress at school and future development. Strategies to help children and young people regain control of their emotions and their behaviour are therefore a central plank in educational and social support packages.

What we feel causes the problems to some extent governs what we feel we should do about them. Although different theoreticians will argue about the causes, there is general agreement that emotional and behavioural problems can originate in the child; can be associated with relationships between parents, children and their families; can be sparked by troubles at school; and can also be triggered by events from the wider world.

As far as possible, interventions suggested in this book will focus on these four areas and will be those that can be undertaken by front-line workers with no specialist mental health training.

How to use this book

The book is in three parts. Part I gives an overview. Chapter 2 gives a brief outline of the causes and consequences of emotional and behavioural problems in children, and Chapter 3 outlines some ideas from young people. In this new edition, we have drawn on some of the research on 'what parents want' in order to help their children.

Part II summarises the key principles in intervention. Chapter 5 is an important chapter and should be read by all those planning an intervention. In particular, it considers the worker's and the client's rights and responsibilities, legal and ethical duties, competence and the need to recognise the limits to what can and cannot be done. It is also important to read Chapter 6 on assessment.

In the diagram showing the outline of this book (Figure 1) it can be seen that that Part I and Part II are recommended as essential reading. Part III looks at interventions and can be read as necessary. Workers may focus on the particular chapter or intervention relevant to their work.

What evidence is there that this strategy is effective?

Not all interventions have been tested sufficiently rigorously for us to have total confidence that an approach 'works' or is, in the true sense, 'evidence-based'. In the text and in the references, the different interventions are labelled with stars according to different levels of evidence. Finding evidence-based solutions to some social problems can be a much harder research task than finding evidence-based solutions to some medical problems.

In the USA there is a much stronger tradition of evidence-based research. In particular there are now excellent websites highlighting programmes that have been extensively tested and found to be effective. These websites include explicit details of how the programmes should be implemented. In some cases – important in our cost-conscious society – the websites give the approximate cost of running the programme. Some of these websites are summarised in Appendix I. Although we cannot be certain that the techniques found to be effective in the USA will be equally effective here, there is much we can learn from these studies. Many of the prevention projects and projects for children at special risk outlined in Chapters 7 and 8 come from the US. Below each are examples of projects in the UK which may not have been so rigorously evaluated, but which appear to replicate some of the key characteristics.

A decision has been made to include some strategies that are based on 'practice experience'. Experienced front-line workers, as was seen from the workshop in Wiltshire, develop their own repertoire of what they consider works. We cannot say these interventions are 'evidence-based' because there has not been enough research to test their effectiveness, but experience indicates that they may be a useful strategy to try. We need to be cautious when using these interventions. In the past some valued social interventions have not only been ineffective, but have actually been harmful.

Interventions to help children and young people are star-coded according to the following levels, and details of the relevant studies are also given in the references.

* *Practice experience.* The examples suggested here are apparently successful interventions used by experienced front-line workers in Wiltshire and interventions found to be effective by the author (Buchanan) in 10 years of experience working in an educational and child psychiatric setting.

** *Descriptive studies.* Two-star interventions are supported by evidence from descriptive studies that the intervention is effective. These studies have no comparison groups or controls so we cannot be sure that other factors (for example, the process of growing up) were not responsible for the changes seen.

*** *Studies with comparison or control groups.* We can be more certain that these approaches are related to particular outcomes. Findings come from the Blueprint and other well-validated programmes from the USA and from the Cochrane and Campbell reviews (web addresses given in Appendix I) and from the small number of research trials into social interventions that have been undertaken in the UK. In addition, findings from longitudinal birth cohorts, such as the National Child Development Study (NCDS), are included among this group. Also included in this are findings from 'meta-analyses' and systematic reviews, which by combining data from different studies can give us greater confidence in the accuracy of the findings. The National Child Development Study (NCDS) is a continuing, multi-disciplinary longitudinal study which takes as its subjects all those living in Great Britain who were born in a particular week in March, 1958. Available at www.data-archive.ac.uk. Information from www.cls.ioe.ac.uk.

Figure 1 **Outline of this book**

ESSENTIAL READING

Causes and consequences
- What is 'normal' and what is a 'problem'?
- Emotional vs. behavioural problems
- Measuring behaviours
- Causes: risk and protective factors
- Resilience

What helps? The views of young people
- Personal factors
- Family factors
- School

What helps? The views of parents
- Ages and stages at which help is wanted
- Drugs and alcohol
- Bullying

Principles in intervention
- Responsibilities of workers
- Specialist services

What works in assessment?
- Choosing the most effective level of intervention
- Individual assessment tools
- Assessment of 'significant others'
- Tools for talking to children and young people

READ AS NECESSARY

Prevention projects
- Targeted perinatal home visiting
- Working with fathers
- Pre-school programmes
- Structured parenting group programmes
- Other interventions
- Peer-led life teaching skills with adolescents
- Telephone/internet helplines

Children at special risk
- Children of substance-abusing parents
- Children experiencing divorce
- Living with domestic violence
- Supporting young carers
- Living with parental mental illness
- Runaways
- Children at risk of suspension from school

Managing children with emotional and behavioural problems age 3–10
- Principles of behavioural/cognitive behavioural interventions
- Particular interventions

Managing common adolescent emotional and behavioural problems
- Feeling down and depressed
- Managing anxiety and fears
- Managing anger
- Loss and bereavement
- Post-traumatic stress disorder
- Substance abuse
- Risk of offending

Why should social workers, teachers and others working in the front-line be concerned about it?

- Children's behaviour is often the presenting problem that initiates a referral to social and other front-line services.
- Emotional and behavioural problems in children have many causes but are more common in children who experience family and other adversities.
- The first task of the social worker is to safeguard the child/children from harm.
- Children often communicate their distress by 'troubled' behaviour.
- Difficult behaviour can place a child at risk of abuse.
- Emotional and behavioural problems in children interfere with school work, affect their life chances, impinge on peer group and family relationships, and may make them more vulnerable to mental and physical health problems in adult life.
- Children's behaviour is often the last straw that leads to family breakdown and, for children who are looked after, placement breakdown.
- Children with emotional and behavioural problems are 'children in need' under the Children Act 1989.

KEY STUDY

The salutary tale of the Cambridge-Somerville study

In this study, boys at high risk of becoming delinquent were randomly allocated to no-intervention or a planned package of social and psychological support. Thirty years later the intervention was found to make a highly significant difference on measures of criminality, alcoholism, psychosis and early death. Those who took part in the social treatment support programme did far worse than those who had not taken part in a treatment programme (McCord, 1992).

Part I
Overview

1 Why are children with troubled behaviour of interest to social workers, teachers and others working on the front-line?

Under the Children Act 1989 children with emotional and behavioural problems are 'children in need'. Local authorities have statutory responsibilities to provide services for individual children in need. A child is considered to be in need if:

- he is unlikely to achieve or maintain, or to have the opportunity of achieving or maintaining, a reasonable standard of health or development without the provision for him of services by a local authority
- his health or development is likely to be significantly impaired or further impaired, without the provision of such services
- he is disabled (Section 17 (10)).

Section 17(11) defines 'development' as physical, intellectual, emotional, social or behavioural development; and 'health' means physical or mental health (Children Act 1989).

Supporting families, the 1998 Green Paper from the Home Office (Ministerial Group on the Family, 1998), recognises that parenting is a challenging job and that most parents get by with a combination of instinct, advice, reading and family support. The Green Paper notes that this is not always enough. Parents often need help to ensure that small problems in a child's behaviour do not grow unchecked into major difficulties. Children with major emotional and behavioural difficulties are often at the centre of the more serious problems in family life.

The re-organisation of children's services

The Department of Health publication, *Child protection – messages from research* (1995a), concluded that social services departments needed to change their thresholds and refocus more services to support children and families in need. In the last five years, some authorities have attempted to solve the problem by bringing together in one service different groupings: children's social services and education; social services and housing; health and social services. Following the Climbie report (Laming et al, 2003) it is likely that there will be further major changes to child protection services.

> Fundamental reform is now needed to pool knowledge, skills and resources to provide more seamless local services for children. I am, therefore, today inviting health and social services and other local services, like education, to become the first generation Children's Trusts. These pilot Children's Trusts will mean local services for children are run through a single local organisation. … In future, services for children must be centred not around the interests of any organisation but around the interests of the child. …
>
> The most effective safety net is prevention. We want to stop children falling into a spiral of ill health, anti-social behaviour or social exclusion, as well as prevent the worst forms of ill-treatment and abuse. We are looking at how we can create a system where children are provided with the most effective preventative services we can develop. Local Preventative Strategies are being put in place by local authorities across England this year, which will draw together all agencies working with children to provide appropriate services. (Secretary of State for Health Alan Milburn, 28 January 2003)

Research shows that parents are more likely to 'step on board' where services are not stigmatised but universal and open access. The government's mapping report (National Family and Parenting Institute, 2001b) represents a first step towards seeing what services are available and where.

Family/child support services

Many of those who are emotionally or behaviourally disturbed are not in touch with social services, yet are identified in schools and in the home as 'troubled or difficult children'. We should not be surprised that such problems are so central in family support work. By the very nature of their work, family support workers deal with families who are experiencing adversities. Children in these families are a high-risk group for emotional and behavioural problems. In a study for Barnardo's, 80 per cent of referrals were either from step-families or lone parents (Buchanan et al, 1995). Psychological problems are strongly associated with family breakdown and families experiencing change. In one study, some 27 per cent of families coming to social services had experienced domestic violence (Buchanan et al, 1995). The figures may be higher in inner urban areas. We know that witnessing family conflict can be as

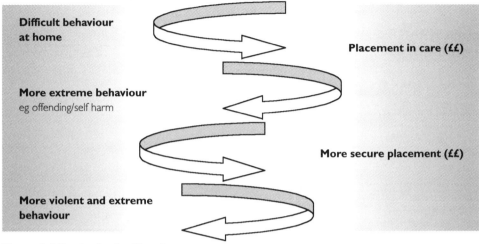

Difficult behaviour at home

Placement in care (££)

More extreme behaviour
eg offending/self harm

More secure placement (££)

More violent and extreme behaviour

Figure 2 **The 'spiral effect'**

disturbing for children as being victims of physical and sexual abuse. Where children are no longer living with their families, placements may break down under the pressure of emotional disturbance.

With older children it is very easy for such disturbance to 'spiral' into more serious problems, such as running away and substance abuse – behaviours that can place children further at risk. It is known that more than one in four children who have been in care have significant levels of maladjustment (Buchanan and Ten Brinke, 1997a). A study in Oxfordshire has shown that more than two thirds of 'looked-after' children have 'clinical' levels of psychiatric illness. The figure for children in residential units may be as high as 96 per cent (McCann et al, 1996). As children move down the spiral not only do their problems escalate, but the cost of caring for them multiplies dramatically, up to an estimated £1,500 per child per week (Children's Legal Centre, 1991).

The increase in children with emotional and behavioural problems

There is considerable evidence that the number of children with 'troubled behaviour' is rising (Rutter and Smith, 1995) and that the heaviest concentration of these children is in the inner urban areas where services are already stretched.

Although more psychiatric and psychological services are required, a report from the Maudsley Hospital (Buchanan and Ten Brinke, 1998) suggests that most children with 'troubled behaviour' need social and educational solutions rather than health intervention. Indeed, the report goes so far as to say that in some cases psychiatric intervention may be counter-productive. Labelling a child a 'psychiatric case' can be more damaging than the disorder itself. The best people to help a 'troubled' child may be those who know the child best. However, if these people are to be effective, they need to learn from evidence-based psychological/psychiatric interventions.

Effective interventions

As children grow up most parents develop a range of strategies to help their son/daughter 'come through' their difficult patch. They recognise that a child has problems in a particular area and find opportunities for the child to develop new skills and/or strategies to divert the child from problematic behaviour. Teachers play an important part in this process. Some children, however, have more difficulty 'coming through'. These may be children who are known to social services.

There is now a range of effective interventions that can be used by front-line workers to help these children. At one level these may be 'compensatory' approaches, very like the sort of things parents do to help their children 'grow out' of their problems. At another level there is a range of group and community projects, some of which have a direct focus on mental health. These projects may offer more specialised help. At a further level there are a range of individual therapies that can be used by front-line workers without specific mental health training.

The ecological framework

In recent years Bronfenbrenner's 'ecological' model (1979)has grown in popularity. This model demonstrates that within the person, the family, the community/school and the wider social environment there are a range of interacting risk and protective factors that can explain different outcomes for children.

At a basic level, this framework helps us understand what may have caused a problem, but more importantly it shows how we can set in place simple 'compensatory' experiences to combat the child's difficulties.

Once a child is presenting with significant emotional and behavioural problems, different theoretical treatment models – for example, psychoanalytic, social learning, family systems – will give very different ideas about how these problems can be remedied.

Some theoretical approaches may not be recommended for a particular problem, indeed they may do harm. Other approaches may just take too long (children 'in need' may not be able to wait for their parents to benefit from therapy) and some may be unacceptable to children and families (they simply do not turn up). Finally, amidst the reality of the world in which we work, recommended treatment may simply not be available.

Workers, mindful of their knowledge, expertise and the limits to their competence, need to choose carefully on the evidence available which approach they use and with whom.

Two principles have governed the recommendations in this book. First, there will be evidence that interventions recommended are effective, and second, the interventions require no, or limited, specialist mental health expertise.

Children with problems

Research by Buchanan using data from the National Child Development Study (NCDS), which has followed a cohort born in one week in 1958, has shown that nearly half of all children have 'difficult' behaviour at some stage in their growing-up period. In this study, children's behaviour was measured at three time points: ages 7, 11 and 16. Around 50 per cent of the children who had difficult behaviour at one age had grown out of it by the next time point four years later. Very few of these children

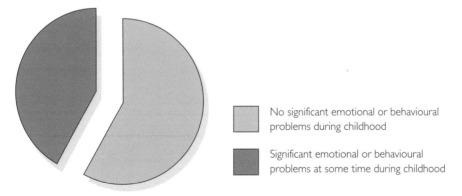

No significant emotional or behavioural problems during childhood

Significant emotional or behavioural problems at some time during childhood

Figure 3 **Children with significant emotional and behavioural problems during childhood**

had formal treatment. It is likely that in most children the natural process of development is responsible for many of these changes but that other children are helped to modify their behaviour by the actions of parents, teachers and friends.

Key messages

- Responding to 'troubled children' is central to family/child support services.
- Numbers of children with emotional and behavioural problems are increasing.
- There is now a range of effective interventions.
- Interventions can be undertaken with the child, his family, school/community and within the wider social policy context.
- Children can, with help, 'recover' from their difficulties.

2 Causes and consequences of emotional and behavioural problems

It might be expected that as living conditions have improved over the course of this century psychosocial disorders in young people would have become progressively less frequent. The evidence from our study firmly contradicts this commonly held assumption. Physical health has improved in line with better living conditions. However, against expectation, psychosocial disorders have shown no such fall in frequency … the evidence suggests that many have become substantially more prevalent. (Rutter and Smith, 1995, p763)

Smith and Rutter examined five problem areas: youth crime and conduct disorders; substance misuse; depressive problems; eating disorders; suicide and suicidal behaviours. In varying degrees, such problems can seriously interfere with the life chances of thousands of young people. Less serious problems also disable children. Indeed it has been shown that emotional and behavioural problems are the most common cause of disability in childhood (Bone and Meltzer, 1978).

SOME POSSIBLE CONSEQUENCES OF EMOTIONAL AND BEHAVIOURAL PROBLEMS

In childhood
- poorer family relationships
- lower levels of school achievement
- greater risk of school suspension/expulsion
- links with offending behaviour
- fewer qualifications
- poorer employment prospects
- social exclusion

In adult life
- poorer relationships with partners and own children
- links with mental health problems in adult life
- possible links with a range of serious physical illnesses

When seeking to help children and young people, the starting point is to decide whether a child/young person has a problem.

What is 'normal' and what is a 'problem'?

The term 'mental health problems' is used to describe a very broad range of emotional or behavioural difficulties, which may cause concern or distress. At one end in this continuum is the child without emotional and behavioural problems (is there such a child?) and at the other end there is a small group of children with considerable problems. Most children fall somewhere in the middle.

Figure 4 **Children's behaviour**

In this book we are focusing on those children who are more distressed and more difficult than other children: those whose difficulties have started to impinge on their family relationships, school work and friendship patterns. At school, the child who is consistently more aggressive than other children stands out. The teenager who fails to get to school (in a school with low truancy rates), breaks the 'normal' pattern of behaviour. As we saw in Chapter 1, emotional and behavioural problems in children are remarkably common. Nearly half of all children have a 'difficult patch' at some stage while they are growing up. A few children suffer long-term harm as a result of short periods of extremely turbulent behaviour. Other children develop a longer-term pattern of emotional and behavioural problems. As family relationships and school work suffer, opportunities and life chances gradually erode.

What is the difference between emotional and behavioural problems?

When children are disturbed, they can react in two ways. Some become sad and depressed. These children are 'internalising' their distress. Although children may first develop an internalising disorder following a difficult time in their lives, some children may be inherently more prone to anxiety and depression than others (Kovacs and Devlin, 1998). Whatever the cause, the distress of these children may be associated with a range of psychosomatic problems such as wetting and soiling. Younger children may become fearful and try to avoid situations they find difficult, such as school. Older children may self-harm or overdose.

Other children may have temper tantrums or become aggressive and start fighting with their friends. These children are acting out or 'externalising' their problems. They can be very hard to manage particularly if they are overactive. This overactivity may be a characteristic of the child but the behaviour becomes more problematic when parents themselves are under pressure. It is very easy for parents to get into a negative cycle.

Children who are constantly 'told off' become negative about themselves and act out their frustration and aggression. They may become progressively more antisocial and may get involved in antisocial activities as they become older.

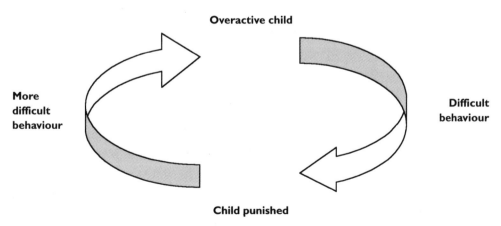

Figure 5 **The negative cycle**

Similarly, children with internalising behaviour may get into a downward negative cycle where each new problem increases their distress and confirms that they cannot cope. The challenge for those at the front-line who are working with children who have internalising or externalising disorders is to reverse the process and start a more positive cycle.

There is also another group of children with *developmental disorders*. These are not considered here. Such children may have developmental delays in speech or language acquisition, or reading delays. There may be learning disability or specific problems such as autism. These children may also have emotional and/or behavioural problems but these may have come as a result of their developmental problems. Children with developmental disorders need specialist help.

Finally, it is important to remember that there are the rarer childhood psychiatric illnesses such as early-onset schizophrenia, anorexia nervosa, Tourette syndrome and many others. These are not considered here and should all be referred for specialist assessment/treatment.

How is behaviour measured?

Professor Sir Michael Rutter was one of the first to develop a checklist of behaviours that identified children with adjustment difficulties. This checklist was developed in 1970 from a survey of all children aged 10 or 11 in the Isle of Wight. Scores on the Health and Behaviour Checklist were then compared to findings from psychiatric assessments on the children (Rutter et al, 1970).

Other checklists have been developed following Rutter's early work. Some of the better known are the Achenbach checklists (***), the Early Years Behaviour Checklist (Barnes and Rickman, 2003), formerly the Pre-School Behaviour Checklist and more recently the Goodman Strengths/Difficulties Questionnaire (SDQ). Achenbach checklists should be administered by those with some psychological training and give a more in-depth assessment. The Goodman SDQ (Goodman 1997b) is particularly popular, and is available in the package of assessment measures from the Department of Health under the *Framework for the assessment of children in need* (2000). It is also available directly from the web (www.sdqinfo.com). The SDQ focuses on what a child is good at, as well as what he/she finds difficult. It is very simple to use and the same proforma can be utilised for all ages from 4–16 and is available in a number of different languages. A similar version is available for children under the age of 4. The checklist can be used by parents or teachers or by young people reporting on their own strengths/difficulties. Scores from these checklists are added up and there is a suggested cut-off point to indicate children with more significant difficulties. More reliable ratings are obtained when parent, teacher and/or child report scores are combined.

THE POSSIBLE PROS AND CONS OF MEASURING BEHAVIOUR USING THE STRENGTHS/DIFFICULTIES QUESTIONNAIRE

Pros

- You learn about the child's strengths as well as the child's difficulties
- You know whether the child or the parent has the problem
- You can tell whether things are getting better
- You can tell if things are getting worse
- It only takes 5–10 minutes

Cons

- You may be 'labelling' the child (perhaps less of a concern than not getting the child the necessary help)
- You may worry the parent (research suggests most parents welcome the opportunity to complete checklists)
- You can't spare the time (the SDQ, unlike some checklists, takes about 10 minutes – it is written in everyday language and can be completed by non-psychologists)

How many children have emotional and behavioural problems?

Different definitions of emotional and behavioural problems, different ages and different areas will give very different figures for the number of children involved. Rutter in the Isle of Wight in the 1970s found that 7 per cent of children had significant emotional and behavioural problems at age 10 and 11. When he repeated his study in inner London using the same assessment measures the rates were more than doubled. In London the rate of disorder for boys was 25 per cent and 13 per cent for girls (Rutter et al, 1975). A national study carried out by the Office for National Statistics (Meltzer et al, 2000) found significant mental disorder in over 10 per cent of young people aged 5–15 years. In the 11–15-year-olds, the rate was 11.2 per cent compared to a rate of 8.2 per cent in the 5–10-year-olds.

It can therefore be calculated that in any secondary school of 1,000 pupils there are likely to be 50 pupils who are seriously depressed and 100 who are suffering significant distress.

Internalising disorders such as depression and anxiety are less common in early childhood and more common in adolescence, particularly among girls. Externalising disorders are common in younger children, particularly among boys. In adolescence the use and abuse of drugs and alcohol is a significant issue: 29 per cent of 13-year-olds report drinking alcohol once a week and 16 per cent of 16-year-olds regularly use solvents or illegal drugs. Children who are looked after in the care system or are care-leavers, who have been excluded from school or are homeless or young carers, are particularly at risk.

Research has also shown that there are very close links between mental health problems in parents and those in children (Falkov, 1998). A depressed mother may not be sufficiently assertive to ask for help. Although seriously depressed parents need psychiatric care, other parents, particularly lone mothers, may be underfunctioning and depressed because of their social situation. As such they may respond to social interventions, for example admission to a family centre. The General Health Questionnaire (GHQ) (Goldberg, 1978) can identify parents who need help before the problem gets too bad.

Risk and protective factors

The 'ecological' model (originating from Bronfenbrenner, 1979) brought together some of the earlier theories. Life history research and findings from longitudinal studies in the UK and elsewhere give support to the model. Broadly speaking, the developing child, whatever his/her genetic inheritance may be, interacts with the different systems with which he or she comes into contact: the child both influences these systems and is influenced by them.

Life history research has shown us that in each domain there is a range of risk factors for emotional and behavioural problems and a range of protective factors – that is, factors that may protect a child from maladjustment.

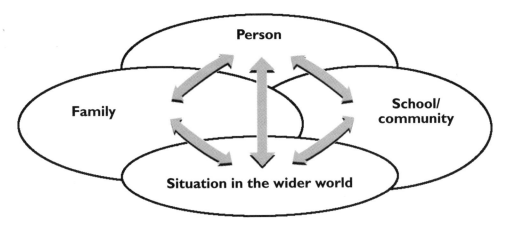

Figure 6 **The ecological framework**

The following summary comes from an extensive review of the literature undertaken by Buchanan (Buchanan and Ten Brinke, 1998)

Although in the past it was tempting to deny the evidence of parents who always maintained that each child in a family was different, a growing number of research studies are now showing a genetic component in both emotional and behavioural disorders. Research into behavioural genetics is growing apace and it is likely that many new developments will emerge, such as Plomin's study on the relationship between genetics and behaviour (Plomin, 2001). The Virginia Twin Study (Eaves et al, 1997) found that virtually all internalising and externalising behaviour shows 'moderate' genetic effects. 'Moderate' effects, however, suggest that environmental factors are necessary for the expression of the disorder:

> We should not lose sight of the fact that the same genetic data provide the best available evidence for the importance of non-genetic factors. Rarely does genetic influence account for more than half of the variance of behavioural dimensions and disorders. (Plomin, 1994)

For those of us who are working with young people, this is a hopeful message. It means that although some children may be biologically more vulnerable to particular problems, we may be able to 'manipulate' the environment so that they are less likely to develop the problem in the first place. We may also be able to adjust the social situations of those who already have problems so that they are more likely to 'recover'.

Table 1 **Risks and protective factors for emotional and behavioural problems**

Factors in the person	Factors in the family	Family in the school/community	Wider world
Risks	Risks	Risks	Risks
• genetic factors making the children more vulnerable to emotional and behavioural problems	• family adversities	• poor reading/low school attainment	• economic recession
	• poverty	• poor rates of achievement in schools	• unemployment
	• mental illness in parents		• housing shortage
• temperament.	• alcoholism, criminality	• bullying in schools	• family change: increasing family breakdown
• impulsiveness	• conflict with, and between parents	• disadvantaged community/ neighbourhood crime	
• physical illness or impairment	• lax inconsistent discipline		• long working hours/job insecurity
• mental disabilities	• punitive, authoritarian/ inflexible parenting	• racial tension/ harassment	
		• an experience of public 'care'	
Protective factors	Protective factors	Protective factors	Protective factors
• biological resilience	• good relationships with parents	• supportive community	• 'inclusive' policies
• good health and development	• supportive grandparents –	• schools with good rates of achievement, good 'ethos', lack of bullying.	
• good problem-solving skills/high IQ	• lack of domestic tensions		
	• family involvement in activities	• opportunities for involvement and achievement	
	• being brought up by birth family		

The importance of parenting style

From parenting research some clear messages have emerged about the importance of parenting style. Some parenting styles are more closely linked than others to emotional and behavioural problems in children. Basically children, whatever their genetic inheritance, have fewer problems when their parents are positive and encouraging but also give them some boundaries. Figure 7 shows how this works. On the one hand is the totally permissive parent, who has no idea what is happening to his/her children when they are out of sight, and on the other hand there is a very rigid, controlling parent who can be very punitive. Across the middle at one end there is the parent who listens and is positive, accepting and supporting, compared to the other extreme where the parent cannot say one nice thing about their child, and is constantly critical of what they do.

When parents get the balance right, this impacts on children's self-esteem, schooling, social acceptance, close friendships, behavioural conduct and self-worth (McClun and Merrell, 1998) and protects them against such problems as drug/alcohol misuse (Cohen et al, 1994). Figure 8 summarises the research findings.

Resilience: the 'X' factor?

A central finding in all the literature on psychosocial adversities is that some children, despite prolonged and severely negative experiences, survive intact. What is this 'X' factor? What can be done to promote resilience? Recent research has taken

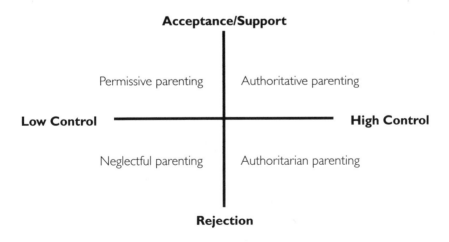

Figure 7 **Four Quadrant Parenting Model**

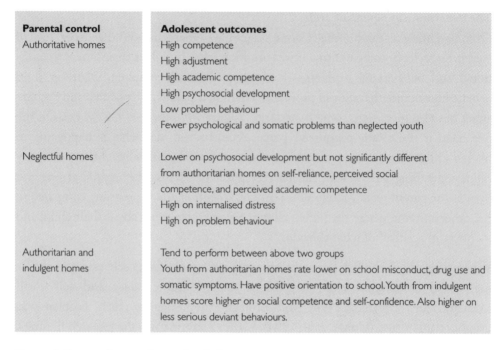

Parental control	Adolescent outcomes
Authoritative homes	High competence
	High adjustment
	High academic competence
	High psychosocial development
	Low problem behaviour
	Fewer psychological and somatic problems than neglected youth
Neglectful homes	Lower on psychosocial development but not significantly different from authoritarian homes on self-reliance, perceived social competence, and perceived academic competence
	High on internalised distress
	High on problem behaviour
Authoritarian and indulgent homes	Tend to perform between above two groups
	Youth from authoritarian homes rate lower on school misconduct, drug use and somatic symptoms. Have positive orientation to school. Youth from indulgent homes score higher on social competence and self-confidence. Also higher on less serious deviant behaviours.

Figure 8 **Parenting style and adolescent outcomes (Lamborn et al, 1991)**

some of the mystery out of resilience. Certainly personal attributes play a part ('the born survivor') but there is also much that can be done to promote resilience. Bruce Compas, in studies on children's coping strategies, has found that one of the biggest threats to children's mental health is the *persistent* presence of minor irritants rather than occasional major stressors (Compas, 1995).

In New Zealand, the Christchurch longitudinal study compared two groups who scored highly on a family adversity index. Assessed at age 15–16, the resilient group had low self-reported offending ratings, police contact, conduct problems, alcohol abuse and school drop-out, whereas the non-resilient group had high ratings on these factors. The first finding was that in this high-risk group, the resilient young people *had significantly lower adversity scores*. Those with multiple problems usually had the highest scores. Resilient young people tended to have higher IQs at 8 years; had lower rates of novelty seeking at age 16; and were less likely to belong to delin-quent peer groups. Girls were no more resilient than boys. There was little difference between the two groups on parental attachment, and other individual features were not linked to the variations in resilience (Fergusson and Lynskey, 1996).

What are the implications of this study? Firstly, even with children who experience multiple adversities, lightening the load may free up energy that can be used productively. Secondly, in adolescence the key influence is not so much the family but the peer group. Common-sense strategies to divert young people away from delinquent peer groups seem to be supported by research.

Rutter (Rutter et al, 1998), in reviewing all the research, hypothesises that resilience in young people may (he feels far from certain) be promoted by:

- reducing sensitivity to risk by giving young people opportunities to succeed in challenging activities
- reducing the impact of the risk by parental supervision; positive peer group experience; avoidance of being drawn into parental conflict; and opportunities to distance oneself from the deviant parent
- reducing negative chain effects resulting, for example, from suspension from school; truancy; drug and alcohol abuse
- increasing positive chain effects by eliciting supportive responses from other people, for example, linking a young person with someone who may help in getting a job
- promoting self-esteem and self-efficacy by giving young people opportunities to succeed in tasks and success in coping with manageable stresses
- compensatory experiences that directly counter the risk effects, for example, where a child has witnessed domestic violence, positive models of non-violent men
- opening up of positive opportunities, for example, through education and career opportunities
- positive cognitive processing of negative experiences, for example, teaching coping strategies and skills, viewing negative experiences positively, being constructive.

To this we might add, some further evidence from Bruce Compas (1995). He describes interventions for promoting coping at three levels: programmes for coping with generic stress, programmes for coping with acute stress and programmes for young people coping with chronic stress. The key components of an effective programme appear to be: giving information about the problem and giving information about the way stress manifests itself; developing rational thinking skills to help problem-solve; and teaching skills in developing effective coping strategies.

As we explore 'what works' in the following chapters, we may ponder whether these components explain why some programmes work and why others are less successful.

Key messages

- Longitudinal research has been helpful in identifying risk and protective factors for a range of human conditions. We know from Rutter and others that clusters of adversities increase the likelihood of problems. A conclusion supported by work on the National Child Development Study (Buchanan et al, 2002) is that clusters of protective factors or 'good experiences' may compensate for clusters of 'bad experiences'.

- The 'X' Factor, 'resilience', may represent something that, as yet, we do not fully understand. Research suggests that so-called 'resilience' may indicate that somewhere along the line a child has had enough good experiences to develop the confidence to cope, and, more controversially, enough challenging experiences to practise and refine the necessary coping strategies. Our task is to build on whatever strengths the young people have and to help them develop the coping skills and strategies that can help them survive and prosper.

- Promoting 'successful coping' during adolescence is an important developing area of research:

  Facilitating the development of a wide range of different types of coping skills that can be used flexibly in response to the diverse stressors of adolescence will play an important role in the promotion of effective coping in the youth of tomorrow. (Compas, 1995)

3 What helps? The views of young people

Girls our age are aware that nothing happens at a click of a finger, you have to work at it – a slow process. We're the ones who can do it. (Katz et al, 1998)

Once upon a time there were men's jobs and women's jobs. Now women are doing men's jobs and men are not doing women's jobs. Once upon a time there were coalminers, things like that. Now it's in decline. (Jake aged 14; Katz et al, 1999)

The exciting recent research on resilience discussed in Chapter 2 suggests that we need to get into young people's heads, or to perceive the world as they see it, if we want to help them.

Reported here are two studies from a national sample that elicited the views of more than 4,000 young people age 13–19 from all over the UK. These views are their perceptions; we do not know whether they relate to what we may call their reality. The girls' study took place in 1996 and the boys' study took place in 1998. For the boys' study, questionnaires were circulated to a control sample in schools to assess the possible newspaper bias. There were few significant differences between the two groups. The young people also give important clues about their coping strategies.

The studies sought to find out:

- how boys and girls with high self-esteem differed from boys and girls with low self-esteem
- what the association was between high/low self-esteem; depression; disaffection from school.

In both the girls' and the boys' study, the sample was divided into two groups of young people at either end of a spectrum. At one end was a group of young people who *felt happy and confident* about themselves; felt that there were exciting opportunities for them; and *got on with their school work* or *set themselves high standards*. These were called the *can-do* group. Between 21 per cent and 25 per cent of young people fell into this group. At the other end were those lacking these characteristics. These were called the *low can-do* group. Between 8 per cent of girls and 13 per cent of boys fell into this group.

Although *low can-do* did not measure emotional and/or behavioural problems as such, there was a very strong relationship with a group of young people who 'often' felt depressed; with young people who were disaffected with school; with young people who were involved with the police; and with a further small group of young people who admitted feeling suicidal (or who had actually made attempts on their lives). The findings are, therefore, of considerable interest to those trying to help young people with emotional and behavioural problems. Some of the findings relating to personal, family and school factors are summarised as follows.

Personal factors

In this study the overall levels of self-esteem were lower in the boys than in the girls. Again this may be part of a changing trend. We know, for example, that in recent years the male youth suicide rate has risen. Among the low self-esteem boys, more than one in ten had attempted suicide. Boys were also concerned about drugs. Overall 85 per cent of boys thought drug use was spreading to younger boys; 60 per cent were worried about the effects on those around them; and 40 per cent worried about the effects on themselves. Surprisingly, low self-esteem boys were significantly less worried about the effects on themselves but *rated drugs highly as a source of stress*.

Bullying in school and violence of one form or another was significantly associated with the low self-esteem. Poignantly, more than 60 per cent of the *low can-do* boys felt they had nowhere to go for emotional support. The *can-do* groups not only had emotional support from mother and in many cases father too, but also their friends and relatives.

Family factors

Around a quarter of all young people worry about conflict in the home, and common across all groups and both genders were worries about parents splitting up and divorcing.

The most significant differences between the *can-do* and *low can-do* groups for both girls and boys related to their families' *parenting style*. As mentioned in Chapter 2, this finding has been consistently reported in a number of studies (summarised in Buchanan and Hudson, 1998). It was interesting that most young people felt their parents were loving. Even in the low self-esteem groups, this was true for more than

60 per cent. The big divide between the *can-do* and the *low can-do* groups came in whether parents offered guidance; were helpful (as seen through the young people's eyes); allowed the young people to make their own decisions; and listened to their problems and views.

Family involvement in their children's lives, or doing things together was another key factor. It may be that spending time with adults doing enjoyable things created the opportunities for talking about things that concerned the young people.

Another group of family characteristics clearly divided the high and low self-esteem boys. This was the relationship between fathers and sons. An involved father was one who spent time with the boy, was interested in his school work, talked through his worries with him and talked to him about relationships.

Boys with involved fathers were also less likely to be alienated from school, less likely to be involved in criminal activities and less likely to be depressed. Steve Biddulph in *Raising boys* (1998) talks about the need boys have for dads and dad-figures. In the US there is research support for the Big Brothers/Big Sisters Program.

DOES MENTORING WORK? AN EVALUATION OF THE BIG BROTHERS/BIG SISTERS PROGRAM

A random assignment evaluation reported that that Big Brothers/Big Sisters mentoring had a significant positive effect on young people age 10–16 years. Over an 18-month follow-up period, 571 youths participating in Big Brothers/Big Sisters Programs were significantly less likely to have started using illegal drugs or alcohol, hit someone or skipped school than 567 controls. They were also more confident about their school performance and got along better with their families. Mentors were carefully screened, trained and matched with a young person whom they met, on average, three or four times a month for approximately a year. The programme also provided professional supervision of these matches (Grossman and Tierney, 1998). Despite this positive evaluation, a review of mentoring schemes in both the UK and US cautions us that the evidence for their effectiveness is based more on positive accounts by participants than by empirical evidence of impact on issues such as a reduction in offending (see www.whatworksforchildren.org.uk).

School factors

Young people's views were also elicited about what happened in the school setting. *Can-do* boys and girls were not necessarily high achievers. In selecting the *can-do* group, measures of high achievement had been deliberately omitted. Although some of the older *can-do* girls and boys were in college or heading for further education, others were working on skills training and a few were on benefit.

Young people who had a good experience at school, regardless of whether they were high achievers, were more likely to belong to the *can-do* group. For some children a good experience at school was related to whether their school had an effective 'anti-bullying' policy.

The overlap between different groups of boys

The study also explored whether the *can-do* and the *low can-do* groups crossed over with other groups of children with problems. As can be seen from Figure 9, under 20 per cent of *can-do* young people were seriously disaffected by school, depressed or in trouble with the police. On the other hand around 70 per cent of the *low can-do* young people had one of the above problems and 11 per cent were disaffected with school, depressed and in trouble with the police.

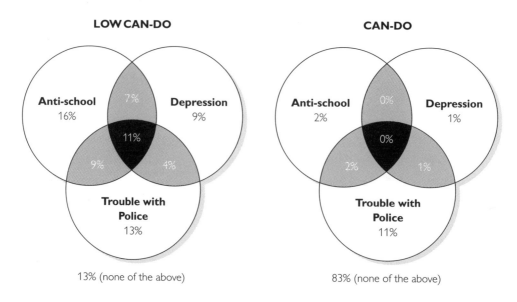

Figure 9 **Venn diagrams of the overlap between different groups of boys**

Key messages

The young people in this study were talking about their particular experiences, but grouped together they have a message for adults involved in teaching or the care of young people which can be summarised as follows.

- If you want to help me, you need to see the world as I see it.
- Many young people worry about family relationships; fear parents breaking up; and are stressed by family conflict. These family difficulties affect how we feel about ourselves and lower our self-esteem. These are everyday stresses for us.
- Those of us who need it most may have less emotional support from parents. We value parents who are positive and yet give some boundaries.
- We feel good about ourselves when parents (these may be step-parents or foster carers) listen, talk about things that concern us and give us guidance. We also feel good about ourselves when we do things together with the family and when fathers or father-figures take an interest in us. But as we get older, we need to learn how to make decisions (this may involve letting us make mistakes).
- We worry about the effects of drugs on others and on ourselves. For some this is an important source of stress.
- Good experiences in school make all the difference to our self-esteem. We need teachers who know us as people; courses that are delivered well; teachers who don't make us feel stupid if we don't understand something; and good career advice.
- More importantly we need schools where we are not bullied, that have anti-bullying policies that work and where we are not threatened with violence.

The other side to the equation – parents' views

The views expressed here by the young people are, of course, only one side of the equation. As we see in Chapter 4, the challenge for workers supporting families with children who have emotional and behavioural problems is also to listen to parents' perceptions of their children's difficulties and to make the bridge between the two worlds.

4 What helps? The views of parents

Listen to parents. Treat individual cases as different. Don't jump to conclusions. (Advice from parent to social worker; Buchanan et al, 2002)

These words encapsulate much good practice as well as current government thinking. The dilemma for those working with parents and their children lies in identifying strategies that will improve outcomes for troubled children but which also work with parents in achieving what they want in an open, supportive and non-judgmental way. Perhaps more importantly, it lies in identifying what parents want rather than imposing programmes upon them. The focus of this chapter is on the parents' concerns with practical information relating to these strategies. Further details of specific interventions for specific problems are given later in the book.

The National Family and Parenting Institute (NFPI, 2001a) organised interviews with 1,391 parents and reported the following key findings.

- Parents' biggest anxiety about family life in Britain is about the risks from drugs and alcohol. This was consistent across men and women, race and social class, but showed variations in different parts of the country.
- Education is a major concern, particularly to parents living in London and eastern England.
- Parents found teenage years the most difficult to handle, but less than half wanted more information to help them through those years.
- Parents' recipe for a successful family life was spending time together and talking with each other – partners as well as children.
- Some parents value and want information about parenting and children, but a substantial number (48 per cent) said they do not require more information about child development.
- Parents are most likely to seek information first from family and friends and then from local services, like their doctor, local school or playgroup.
- Other sources of information, including government sources, were less popular.

After drug and alcohol use, parents' second biggest worry was about their children's behaviour. In a similar vein, the Home Office's Parenting Policy Forum found that parents were particularly concerned about the prevalence of drugs in schools, the impact of divorce on their children, support with parenting teenagers and bullying. One clear message from both reports is that parents do not want to be told how to parent, particularly by the government. As the NFPI (2001a) concludes:

> One clear message for both the statutory and voluntary sectors is that one size does not fit all; that the way that information is communicated is at least as important as the content; and that most parents would prefer to rely on informal, local networks for support than more distant and formal services.

Parents who are already receiving services

Research with 70 parents already receiving services from social services in Wiltshire suggests that some parents want support not only for their children, but also for themselves and their family (Buchanan et al, 2002). Strategies to help parents manage problems and conflict and deal with depression may be helpful. Many lone parents are not depressed in the clinical sense, but may need more social support and opportunities to meet with others.

Family support workers need to remember that parents who are depressed may be less assertive in asking for services than parents who are not depressed. It can be helpful to check out levels of functioning by using the General Health Questionnaire (GHQ) (Goldberg, 1978).

Figure 10 **What parents in touch with social services wanted**

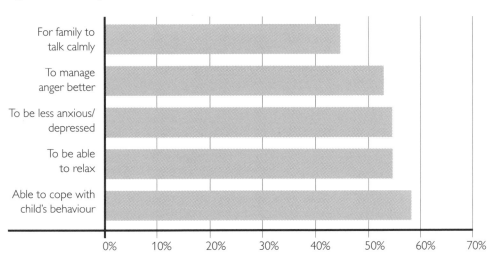

Ages and stages at which parents wanted help

An audit by the NFPI (2001b) found that there was a marked concentration of support services for parents of children under 5, with a gap in provision for older children, and particularly for teenagers. Table 2 (adapted from NFPI, 2001a) shows, however, that parents found the teenage years the most difficult.

All parents go through difficult and tempestuous times with their children. Research with parents suggests, however, that parents do not want advice from the government on how to parent (Home Office, 2000a), are not keen on information about child development (only 15 per cent, for example, wanted more information about the early teenage years although 32 per cent found them difficult) and prefer to use the support and advice of friends and relatives where possible. Recent government consultation on the mapping of services suggests that where possible, services to parents should be non-stigmatising, open-access services provided on a universal basis.

Parenting teenagers

Although about 75 per cent of adolescents have reasonably happy, pleasant relationships with their parents, over 50 per cent of calls to Parentline are from parents of teenagers. Research suggests that day-to-day conflicts over mundane matters are unimportant to teenagers, but are a significant source of distress to parents (Steinberg and Steinberg, 1994). Parents and adolescents bring different sets of expecta-

Table 2 **Which ages and stages of child development a) parents found difficult and b) needed more information about (1,391 respondents)**

	Difficult %	More information %
Conception and pregnancy	4	6
Birth and following month	11	11
Up to a year	8	6
1–5 years	15	7
5–10 years	7	4
Early teenage 11–14	32	15
Late teenage 15–18	27	14
None of these	19	48
Don't know	2	4

tions and social conventions to the table (Steinberg, 2000). Parents can be quite worn down by these adolescent conflicts at a time when they may be experiencing lowered self-esteem, diminished life satisfaction, increased anxiety and depression as they approach middle age.

What can parents do?

- Practise positive, authoritative parenting: encourage and permit the adolescent to develop their own opinions and beliefs.
- Avoid 'psychological control', or 'emotional blackmail'.
- Do not feel you need to show a united front: it's better to have one warm, firm, involved parent than two angry or neglectful parents (Fletcher et al, 1999).
- Avoid conflict at times of greatest stress.
- Maintain channels of communication by listening, supporting, discussion.
- Hang on in there. Most teenagers come through and turn out responsible and reasonable adults!

Support around family breakdown

Today some 30–50 per cent of school-age children experience the break-up of their families in the UK, Canada and the USA (Pagani et al, 1997). Even where conflict is minimal, children and adolescents may experience distress, anger, depression, anxiety, resentment and an acute sense of loss. This often comes when the resident parent, in dealing with their own distress, is feeling unable to function normally.

Family breakdown brings with it other problems that affect both the parents' and children's well-being. Divorce or separation often leads to reduced financial circumstances and the stresses associated with moving home and school. Five years after divorce, families have been found, on average, to be living on half the level of income of intact families (Weiss, 1984). One important consequence of divorce or separation may be disruption of the family network and support systems. Although the vast majority of children and young people survive parental separation, about 30 per cent of adolescents find great difficulty in adjusting (Westman, 1983). Family breakdown may affect adolescents' relationships with their parents and lead to a reduction of the child's trust in their parents, combined with an increasing sense of anger which is directed at them (Fine et al, 1983). Continuing parental conflict after separation can raise adolescents' levels of anxiety and lower their levels of self-esteem and control (Buchanan et al, 2001).

What can parents do?

It is important that parents try to reduce conflict between themselves and the adolescent. Where domestic violence exists steps may need to be taken to ensure the parent and children are protected.

HOW TO HELP CHILDREN FOLLOWING FAMILY BREAKDOWN

Parentline Plus (www.parentlineplus.org.uk) suggests:

*   provide opportunities for them to talk
*   listen
*   be honest
*   co-operate
*   keep in contact
*   be patient
*   reassure them
*   give them time
*   involve them in the decsions about the family but don't involve them in arguments.

Parentline Plus has some helpful materials for parents who are separating/divorcing and the National Family and Parenting Institute also publish some useful leaflets (www.nfpi.org.uk).

Although many children live happily in their new families, the arrival of a new step-parent can put extra strain on both children and parents. As most children live with their birth mothers, the mother/child interaction can be pivotal. Knowing what is 'normal' in reconstituted families can help parents to cope with ensuing difficulties and to avoid the pitfalls. Where the children live with a mother who remarries, the mother/child relationship can deteriorate. Compared to first marriages, mothers in step-families have been found to be more negative towards their children in the early stages, and to get into conflicts more often (Dunn et al, 1998; Bray and Berger, 1993).

Children also often show more negative behaviour towards mothers following remarriage (Vuchinich et al, 1991). With young children, relationships tend to improve over time but may deteriorate again in adolescence.

There is some evidence, however, that where step-families involve remarriage in mid-adolescence, outcomes are more positive (Buchanan et al, 1996).

Parentline Plus has some particularly helpful leaflets around some of the difficulties of step-parenting (www.parentlineplus.org.uk) as do the National Family and Parenting Institute (www.nfpi.org.uk). Many of these can be downloaded direct from the web.

Whether parents separate or divorce, most young people will experience loss. When a parent dies, however, the loss, though far deeper, is less conflictual. Generally, outcomes for those who experience the death of a parent are better than for those who experience parental separation. Other researchers also note that bereavement does not have the same implications for poorer educational attainment, socio-economic disadvantage and psychological problems as separation and divorce have (Rodgers and Pryor, 1998).

Many people experiencing bereavement have found contact with Cruse helpful (www.crusebereavementcare.org.uk).

The importance of family time together
The National Family and Parenting Institute found that most parents would describe a successful family as one that shares time together, and this is strongly supported by research. Studies from the west of Scotland have shown that 'families who do things together' ('family togetherness') are less likely to have adolescents who are involved in a range of problem behaviour such as substance abuse (Sweeting and West, 1995).

We live in a cash-rich, time-poor society with more than 50 per cent of those with children under 5 working, albeit often part-time (NFPI, 2001a) Where joint incomes are low, parents have the added burden of housework and childcare that is outsourced, for example, to childminders and nurseries, which in turn necessitates extra time spent in collecting the children. Government initiatives to make work practices more family-friendly reflect recognition of the growing strain on families, particularly those with young children. Yet the UK still lags behind the rest of Europe in the provision of state nursery care for the under 5s, suggesting that until more action is taken at a social policy level to improve universal provision for the under 5s, lack of shared time together will remain, for most, the reality. The National Family and Parenting Institute publish some useful leaflets on the work/life balance (www.nfpi.org.uk).

When children are involved in drugs and alcohol

Although most parents worry about their children's involvement in drug and alcohol use, some comfort may be taken both from the relatively late average onset of drug use in the UK, and from the evidence that the vast majority of young people using Class B (soft) drugs do not go on to become Class A (hard) drug users, or to become involved in crime (Pudney, 2002).

WHO TAKES WHAT AND WHEN?

- Substances with earliest onset, at around age 14: alcohol, tobacco and glue/solvents
- mean age of onset of cannabis use: 16.6
- mean age of onset for LSD, magic mushrooms: 17.3
- mean age of onset for amphetamines and heroin: 17.7
- mean age of onset for crack: 18.4
- mean age of onset for ecstasy: 18.9
- mean age of onset for cocaine: 20.2

Parents tend to worry about lifestyles that they feel may threaten their child's future either physically, mentally or materially. But generally the evidence suggests that concerns need to go wider than drug use itself. A Home Office study (Pudney, 2002) found the following.

- Problematic behaviour precedes drug abuse. The average ages of onset for truancy and crime are 13.8 and 14.5 years respectively, compared with 16.2 years for drugs generally and 19.9 years for any hard drugs.
- Social, economic and family circumstances seem to be the dominant influences on young people's risk of becoming involved in crime and drug use.
- Indirect policies aimed at problems of local deprivation and family breakdown may offer at least as much hope as more direct anti-drug and anti-crime policies.
- 'Gateway effects' from soft to hard drugs are probably very small.
- Early onset of drug use is associated with later high-risk behaviour, including hard drug use and volume of drug/alcohol use.

Who is most at risk?

The homeless, runaways, those in care, the abused, those whose parents use drugs and those with behaviour disorders are, in general, more vulnerable to early onset drug use and progression to problem drug use. They often have a range of problems, of which drug use is one. Responses need to be comprehensive.

Interventions for those at most risk need to be early, intensive and sustained over time, and demand good inter-agency working (eg, schools, pupil referral units, GPs, health professionals, youth justice).

What can parents do?

Parents need to be aware that 'the role of parents is crucial' (Advisory Council on the Misuse of Dugs, 1993). Communication is more important than condemnation. Today, experimenting with soft drug and alcohol use can be seen as a relatively 'normal' part of growing up. Parental style is important. Negative, neglectful and harsh parenting is associated with vulnerability to a range of childhood and adolescent disorders, such as emotional and behavioural problems, as well as to problems of early onset drug and alcohol use. Parents who are involved in drug misuse themselves will find it much harder to prevent their children being involved.

Parents may need help in developing their parenting skills and channels of family communication. They also need information about drugs and drug misuse to improve communication about drugs with their children. Useful information on a wide range of drugs is available at www.trashed.co.uk.

Access to drugs

The Parenting Policy Forum noted parents' concern about the use and availability of drugs in school. The ease with which young people can access illegal drug markets is likely to be a substantial factor in whether they begin and continue to use drugs. Home Office figures suggest that 68 per cent of young people find cannabis very easy or fairly easy to get hold of, but that only 20 per cent find heroin, and 24 per cent crack, very or fairly easy to get hold of (Aust et al, 2002).

Parents can work closely with schools to urge them to take action against dealers both within schools and at the gates, thus limiting access to drugs for a substantial proportion of the day.

When children are being bullied

How serious a problem is it?

The Damilola Taylor tragedy where a young boy of 10 was left bleeding to death, having been allegedly attacked by a gang of other children from his community, reminds us of the horror of what children can do to each other.

Bullying, as we saw in the Chapter 3, is widespread. In the UK, 27 per cent of junior and middle school pupils and 10 per cent of secondary school pupils said that they had been bullied sometimes or more often during that term. A further 10 per cent and 4 per cent respectively said that they were bullied more than once a week (Chesson, 1999). The national anti-bullying campaign helpline receives 16,000 calls every year from distressed pupils (Chesson, 1999).

Who does it happen to?

Problem behaviours, attitudes towards deviance, peer influences, depressive symptoms, school-related functioning and parenting have all been found to distinguish between those who have never been bullied or victimised and those who are either victims, bullies or bully-victims.

- *The victim*: tends to be more anxious and depressed, socially isolated, with low self-esteem, and to be physically weak or non-assertive (Perry et al, 1988; Craig, 1998). There is some research to suggest victims are also more likely to experience violence in the home (Katz et al, 2000).
- *The bully*: is associated with a punitive parental discipline style, and negative peer influences (Espelage et al, 2000). These children often come from violent homes, bringing what they have learnt at home about solving problems into the schools and then practising their violence on the streets.
- *The bully-victim*: Many bullies also report being victims (Haynie et al, 2001). Bully-victims have been found to have lower scores than other students for scholastic competence, global self-worth, conduct and physical appearance (Mynard and Joseph, 1997).

What are the risks?

- Bullying other children is one of the major causes of exclusion from school; 30 per cent of exclusions are due to bullying, fighting and assaults on peers; 15 per cent of exclusions are due to verbal abuse to peers (Social Exclusion Unit, 1998).

- Depression and suicidal behaviour and suicide are associated with being bullied.
- Bullies tend to report being unhappy with school.
- Bullies often come from families where bullying and force rather than negotiation are the way of solving disagreements.

What can parents do?

The first step is to recognise that your child may have a problem either as a victim or a bully. Michelle Elliot (1991) lists the following indications that a child or young person is being bullied.

> ## SIGNS THAT A CHILD OR YOUNG PERSON IS BEING BULLIED
>
> Children or young people may:
>
> - be frightened if walking to or from school
> - be unwilling to go to school and make continual excuses to avoid going
> - beg to be driven to school
> - change their route to school every day
> - begin doing poorly in their school work
> - regularly have clothes or books or school work torn or destroyed
> - come home hungry (because dinner money was taken)
> - become withdrawn
> - start stammering.

Where a child is being bullied, the first stage is to work together with the school to try to solve the problem. Some schools have introduced home-school agreements, clarifying responsibilities and expectations from both parties with respect to combating bullying (Department for Education and Employment, 1999a).

Other schools now have a 'whole-school approach' to combat bullying. This involves the whole school and parents and the wider community (Besag, 1989; Roland and Munthe, 1989). A whole-school approach towards bullying should make it difficult for bullying – once detected or reported – to continue, as the combined forces of school, parents and the community are there to ensure that it is simply not tolerated.

By setting up a whole-school approach to eliminating bullying, you are sending signals to the children that you do care about their welfare. This approach assumes good pupil-staff relations and creates an atmosphere which continues to foster those relationships. Involving parents and the community will help to change attitudes which encourage bullying. (Elliot, 1991)

Parentline Plus has some useful leaflets to help parents deal with this difficult problem (www.parentlineplus.org.uk).

End note

When a child is troubled and a parent is struggling, it is tempting for those outside the family to think that what the parent, often synonymous with the mother, needs is a good parenting programme to teach them the skills to parent more effectively. The following quote from an earlier publication is a useful reminder.

Working with parents is like walking on eggs. The challenge is to support parents without fracturing their already fragile confidence. Add poverty, poor housing, racism, and all the other stresses that disadvantaged families face, surviving is hard enough without well-meaning professionals telling parents where they are failing.

This then is the starting point for working with families. Whatever their additional problems, parents are parents first with the guilt and anxieties of all parents. If we are to help them we need to obtain their trust that they are safe to share with us the most intimate parts of their life. (Buchanan, 2000)

Key messages

- Parents need to be heard.
- Parents should be encouraged to listen to their children and to open up channels of communication.
- Often parents want support not only for their children but also for themselves and their family.
- Parents should be alert to bullying, and seek help as soon as possible.
- Parents with teenagers are particularly 'stretched'.
- Where there is divorce or separation, the use of mediation and conflict resolution should be encouraged wherever possible.

- Depressed parents may be less assertive, and may not be heard.
- Services to parents should be non-stigmatising, open access services provided on a universal basis
- The most effective parenting is authoritative – warm and affectionate, with boundaries that are negotiated and explained.

Part II
Assessment

5 Principles in intervention

Good practice in providing services should be guided by the rights and needs of clients, the clinical realities and knowledge of possible health gain from intervention, rather than service demands or idiosyncratic practices. Providing quality services to young people means facing a variety of challenges. These include identifying priorities and balancing the conflicting needs and expectations of patients, families and professional groups. There will be a continuing debate about the most effective ways of applying these principles in practice. (Health Advisory Service, 1995)

The reality for most children is that even when they have psychiatric symptoms that result in significant social impairment or distress, only a minority receive any specialist mental healthcare. Research shows that those who do get treatment are more likely to have parents who press for help (Goodman and Scott, 1997, p35). For the vast majority of children with emotional and behavioural problems, the best help they can get is from those front-line workers with whom they are in touch. Given their lack of specific mental health training, it is important that front-line workers have an understanding of their rights and responsibilities; the limits of their competence when they need to pressurise for more specialist help; and the therapies most likely to be successful.

Responsibilities of workers

Respecting the rights and needs of clients

Children, young people and their families have a right to expect the following from the professionals helping them (adapted from 138 and 141, Health Advisory Service, 1995):

- that advice should be available at an early stage
- that their views are heard and respected and that their agreement is sought in the process of assessment and care
- that they are guaranteed confidentiality within relevant legal constraints
- that they are able to participate in interventions which are open, visible and clear

- that they receive feedback and the opportunity to comment
- that they are treated in a manner which affirms the rights and responsibilities of parents
- that they receive interventions from workers that are sensitive to the issues of discrimination and the variety of forms they can take
- that the worker is competent to undertake the intervention.

Legal obligations

Professionals involved with children and young people with emotional and behavioural problems and their families also need to be aware of their legal obligations to their clients. In particular, the law relating to the following (adapted from 138 and 141, Health Advisory Service, 1995):

- *consent to treatment* : Mental Health Act 1983, Code of Practice; Children Act 1989
- *restriction of liberty*: Children Act 1989; Mental Health Act 1983
- *identification and assessment of special educational needs*: Education Acts 1993 and 2002 and Code of Practice
- *disabled people*: Disabled Persons Representation and Consultation Act 1986 (in particular Sections 5 and 6, which relate to support to be provided by social services departments to school leavers with disabilities and special needs); Carers and Disabled Children Act 2000, which covers assessment
- *assessment and Pathway plans for children leaving care*: Children (Leaving Care) Act 2000
- *after-care, mental health opinions in court and the availability of legal advice*
- *complaints procedures.*

Ethics and values

Each profession working with distressed or disturbed children and young people and their families is guided by its own ethical code of practice. In social work, for example, basic to the profession is the commitment to:

> The recognition of the value and dignity of every human being, irrespective of origin, race, status, sex, sexual orientation, age, disability, belief or contribution to society. (Watson, 1985)

Common to all the caring professions is the concept of 'do no harm'.

Competence

Those working with emotionally and behaviourally distressed young people have a commitment to their own professional development. They should be aware of what tasks they are competent to undertake, where they need more knowledge and training before they become involved and what tasks they are not competent to undertake.

The Health Advisory Service advocates that mental health services should be provided in four tiers. The focus in this book is on those offering Tier One and, in some cases, Tier Two services. The vast majority of children with emotional and behavioural disorders will be the responsibility of front-line workers providing Tier One services.

Tier One services

EXAMPLES OF TIER ONE CASES

All cases can turn out to be more complex than they at first appear. The following case examples from experienced social workers appear to be appropriate to Tier One expertise. Cases should be referred on to more specialist care provided in the other tiers if they become more complex.

'Lone parent at end of her tether … Can't get children age 6 and 7 to bed at night.'

'Three-year-old boy has severe behavioural difficulties that seem to be worse with his mother.'

'Fifteen-year-old with minor disability suffered severe bullying at school. Now very withdrawn.'

'Fifteen-year-old girl becoming out of control at home. She is verbally and physically assaulting mother.'

Tier One knowledge and skills (Health Advisory Service, 1995)
- Empathetic interviewing and counselling skills.
- A working knowledge of child development.
- An up-to-date knowledge of child and family problems and disorders.

- An understanding of how major events impact on children's lives, for example, abuse, bereavement.
- An awareness of how the professional's own life experiences inform their approach to others
- familiarity with manifestations of serious or potentially serious psychiatric disorders.

Children whose emotional and behavioural problems involve more risk, are more complex, persistent or whose problems are seriously interfering with social functioning and development should be referred on to Tier Two services.

Tier Two services

Tier Two services are led by professionals with more specialised skills in assessment and interventions. These workers will have some specialist training and may work in social services or educational settings, or as pupil support teachers. Some Tier Two professionals may work in community-based projects catering for 'troubled' children and young people. The following examples also come from experienced social workers.

EXAMPLES OF TIER TWO CASES

'Thirteen-year-old, previously abused in care, constantly running away from home and missing school.'

'Following domestic violence mother and three children lived in a refuge. Mother and children severely traumatised by experiences. School concerned about the children's progress.'

'Mrs X refused to have son home when he was excluded from residential school because of his difficult behaviour.'

'XY referred to us two years ago when his foster placement broke down due to difficult behaviour.'

Tier Two skills include:

- special interview techniques suitable for eliciting information from all age groups

- knowledge of family, group and system dynamics and how these affect individuals in them
- sufficient knowledge and ability to apply some psychologically based therapies.

Cases that are too risky or complex for the Tier Two level of expertise should be referred on to Tier Three services.

Tier Three services

Tier Three services are offered by teams of staff working in specialist child and adolescent mental health services who have the training and facilities to offer increasingly more sophisticated assessment and therapeutic interventions. Such cases may involve eating disorders, substance misuse, developmental disorders such as autism and delays in acquiring skills, depression and self-harming behaviours.

EXAMPLES OF TIER THREE CASES

(ADAPTED FROM HEALTH ADVISORY SERVICE, 1995)

'Michael was a 4½ -year-old boy who had rather odd speech and who did not respond to simple behaviour modification measures. He had a number of developmental delays that suggested he may need special school. Mother was quite markedly depressed.'

'Paul was a 13-year-old boy whose biological mother had been unable to care for him and who had spent much of his early life in foster homes. At the age of 8 Paul was adopted but his behaviour was problematical. Eventually his adoptive father assaulted him and he had to be removed from the family.'

In the second example above, experienced workers in a resource centre in Wiltshire felt that this case would, probably, have been treated by them rather than by more traditional Tier Three services. In different areas, there may be some flexibility between Tier Two and Tier Three cases, depending on the expertise and resources available.

Finally, there are Tier Four services which offer very specialised in-patient and out-patient services and are staffed by those with extremely specialised skills.

Tier Four services

EXAMPLE OF A TIER FOUR CASE

(ADAPTED FROM HEALTH ADVISORY SERVICE, 1995)

'Alastair, aged 14, slowly became uninterested in school, socially withdrawn and isolated. He was uncharacteristically aggressive to his parents ... he felt he was 'under surveillance' and he noticed that a lot of furniture had gone missing from school. His parents were frightened of him and felt unable to care for Alastair. On assessment the psychiatrist diagnosed a psychotic illness and he was admitted to a specialist unit.'

Engaging the child and the family

The key task for anyone trying to help children with emotional and behavioural problems and their families is to engage with them. Case examples from experienced social workers vividly illustrate the issues.

As we see in the examples below, the key to successful outcomes is a good working relationship with parent/s. Parents are 'experts' in their own children, they are also responsible for them before the law (unless *parental responsibility* is shared with others). Similarly, with adolescents, a good working relationship with the young person is essential. A familiar challenge for those working with adolescents is arbitrating in a stormy relationship between parent and young person.

Good working relationships are built on trust, respect, a non-judgmental approach, empathy, openness, honesty, competence and genuineness (see the research in this area summarised in Egan, 1990). This does not mean that a good working relationship on its own is enough: it is simply the vehicle that keeps potentially effective interventions on the road.

In Chapter 6 there is a discussion on 'motivational interviewing'. This has proved a useful tool when working with problem drinkers and substance abusers but may also have wider uses.

Unsuccessful cases – reasons for failure	Successful cases – reasons for success
Father refused to engage in family work	Working in partnership with parents, sharing responsibility and power. Negotiated action-based assessment
Child unable to respond to overtures from resource centre worker, social worker, school etc … Mother unable to reinforce with child what we were trying to do because of poor relationship. No extended family support	Practical services available from community living team who made good relationship with mother … parents' willingness to make it all work
Young person has been unable to use social worker as parents undermined work done on unit	Good working relationship between child's mother, social worker, and foster carer; a general commitment on part of child's family to work with social services to improve the situation
Lack of success due to inability to engage father	Mother and children able to accept intervention and help

Specialist services

When referring cases for more specialist help, it is important to have an overview of the type of service provided by the agency and match that with what is generally known about treatment efficacy. If, for example, a child is likely to need medication, that child needs to be referred to an agency that can prescribe medication such as a GP or a psychiatrist. If family therapy is likely to be the most effective treatment, the child and family need to be referred to an agency that provides this model of treatment.

Goodman and Scott in *Child psychiatry* (1997) give examples of effective and ineffective *child psychiatric* treatments. They base their views on findings from treatment trials and meta-analyses (the pooling of results from a number of trials). More recent findings may give a slightly different picture.

Examples of effective and ineffective treatments (Goodman and Scott, 1997, p229)

There is extensive and sound evidence for the effectiveness of:
- medication in hyperkinesis (extreme over-active behaviour)
- parent training in childhood conduct disorder
- behavioural methods in soiling and enuresis.

There is reasonably sound evidence for:
- cognitive behavioural therapy for adolescent depression
- behavioural approaches for school refusal
- home visiting schemes for physical maltreatment
- family therapy for anorexia when nutritional stability has been achieved.

There is evidence that the following have little or no effect or are harmful:
- unfocused family work for conduct disorder
- social skills therapy given in clinic settings for peer relationship problems
- social work and general support for delinquency.

Psychiatrists note that effective treatments need not necessarily focus on the cause of the problem:

> It is not necessary to treat fire with fire; it is sometimes appropriate to fight fire with water. Medication may help a child's hyperactivity even if that hyperactivity is due to being raised in a grossly inadequate orphanage. (Goodman and Scott, 1997)

In some cases pharmacological treatments may be the best option for some children and young people with mental health problems. The worker has a responsibility to facilitate this by helping the family or young person make contact with his or her GP.

Inter-agency working

Complex problems may need complex solutions. This point is again aptly illustrated by the case vignettes from Wiltshire social workers.

Unsuccessful cases – reasons for failure	Successful cases – reasons for success
Inability to get to grips with the different layers of problems: domestic violence, medical, financial etc surrounding the child's problems	Joint work between social worker and resource centre worker (RCW) including planning + consultation. Work with oldest boy on his own by RCW
Decision to move girl was taken after two years of family support. Respite care was not enough, family situation too complex and too far gone	Several agencies working together; each worker trusting the others, knowing their roles but sharing information. Knowing that it is good enough not to expect rapid change
Child pulled by peer group; no extended family support; family dynamics very destructive	Finding childminder and respite care; joint working with mental health team; family befriender
Young person still misses school; often nights out of the unit; lack of trust due to abuse in care	Individual work with mother improved confidence; work with children helped them express their feelings and anxieties; practical help

Choosing the most effective treatment package/programme
Finally, effective interventions are based on choosing the treatment approach most likely to succeed. Central to this are effective assessments, which is the topic of the next chapter.

Key messages

- Professionals should respect the rights and needs of clients and be aware of their legal obligations to their clients.
- Professionals should be clear about whether or not they are competent to undertake a task.
- Intervention should be matched to the need.
- Good working relationships are built on trust, respect, a non-judgemental approach, empathy, openness, honesty, competence and genuineness.

6 What works in assessment?

> The applied use of risk and protective factors in prevention programmes is sometimes described as an evidence-based approach. It argues that an understanding of relevant factors can not only guide us towards the types of intervention that are likely to prove effective, but can also be used as a practical tool for assessing priorities and identifying overlaps and gaps in existing services. (Utting, 1998)

The first task of an assessment is to decide where to intervene. David Utting in the Cross Departmental Review on Provision for Young Children (1998) notes that reducing risk and enhancing protection in children's lives demands both *multi-agency* and *multi-level* responses.

Local authorities in England and Wales have a duty not only to care for individual children 'in need', but also to identify all children who may be 'in need' in their area. Current government initiatives to combat 'social exclusion', such as Sure Start, the Children's Fund/On Track and Connexions foster this wider community approach.

Choosing the most effective level of intervention

At the community level, the aim is to provide services that are expected to improve children's emotional and behavioural well-being and to strengthen family functioning. Before you can put services in place you have to have some idea of the likely needs.

KEY STUDY

Flintshire Primary Care Service for children

In Wales, Barnardo's was a partner in a pilot service that started in 1996. It involved child psychiatry, child psychology, social work, education and voluntary agencies (Appleton and Hammond-Rowley, 2000). Aware that secondary care services were exercised to the full in work with complex and severe psychological disorders, it was decided that efforts needed to be made to strengthen primary care mental health services in one disadvantaged area, and to help families address difficulties at an early stage.

In the first part of the project a mental health needs assessment of children under 8 was undertaken. This involved consulting a cross-section of parents and professionals about their perceptions of need and a behavioural screening programme. Following the needs assessment, a controlled trial began to examine whether a primary-care-based intervention tailored to the specific community could reduce mental health problems in young school-age children. Measures were taken of three cohorts (200 children in nursery school, 200 children in reception class and 300 in year one) at three time points over three years. While longitudinal data indicated no change at a population level, the number of children for whom concern was expressed by teachers in reception classes halved in the intervention group, and increased in the control group (Appleton et al, 2000, p 59).

Another approach to needs assessment is to use census data or Geographical Information Systems (GIS) (this approach was recommended by Pinnock as part of local authority strategic planning of services for children in need, at the University of Leicester Needs Assessment Conference in September 1998), to create a map to highlight communities in need (Noble and Smith, 1994).

Noble and Smith have developed expertise in this area of work and have developed the Index of Local Deprivation (ILD) for Scotland, Wales and Northern Ireland for the Department of the Environment Transport and the Regions. These are constantly being developed; the most recent publication is *English indices of deprivation 2004* (Noble et al, 2004).

Needs assessment is central in the Communities that Care (CTC) initiative for reducing antisocial behaviour among young people. This project was devised by researchers at the University of Washington, Seattle and has been described as 'one of the most promising strategies to emerge from America' (Farrington, 1996). It is now being adapted for the UK. The starting point is a needs audit of local risk and resources. Interventions can then be targeted on the risk and protection factors identified using a range of strategies of proven effectiveness.

COMMUNITIES THAT CARE RISK AND RESOURCES AUDIT

The underlying assumption of CTC is that the presence or absence of particular factors in a community contribute to the level of youth crime, drug and alcohol abuse, school-age pregnancy, AIDS and school failure. In order to reduce problem behaviours in young people it is necessary to undertake a 'risk and resources audit' so that interventions can be targeted effectively. This involves key leaders from the community and representatives from local agencies in the collection of both 'archival' and 'survey' data to identify local risk and resources and to agree an action plan.

- *Archival data* (the UK equivalents of the original US indicators are given here) relates, for example, to the number per population of alcohol and tobacco sales outlets; local authority rented properties; voters; unemployed; children on free school meals; lone parents; children 'looked after'; children leaving school with no qualifications; divorces; adult arrests for domestic violence; offences involving alcohol-related crime; personal and property crime; juvenile arrests for alcohol-related crime, drug-related crime, violent crime, property crime and vandalism; suicide and adolescent pregnancies; and school drop-outs.
- *Survey data* includes all young people in school in the area; a random telephone survey of parents and adults; and another random survey of young people not in school. Questions cover alcohol, tobacco and drug behaviour and knowledge, delinquency and crime.

Obtaining the 'bench' markers

Crucial to any assessment is to obtain a 'baseline' against which change can be measured. In the Flintshire project, behavioural scores of individual children assessed by both parents and teachers are used as a starting point.

In the Communities that Care project the risk indicators in the community are used as 'performance indicators' to demonstrate whether the projects that have been put in place have produced the desired result. For example, a reduction in school exclusions, an increase in educational attainment, a reduction in the number of children with emotional and behavioural problems or a reduction in youth offending.

This approach, along with others, has been used to monitor change in some of the new government initiatives to combat 'social exclusion' such as the Sure Start programme. If the chosen performance indicators show a positive change, we cannot be completely sure that the change is the result of the interventions. Similarly, if the performance indicators show a negative change, this may be due to other factors. In the Flintshire project, however, we can compare the results from the intervention group with those from the control group who also live in a disadvantaged area. Since the control group will not receive the community-based intervention, any differences seen between the two groups could be attributed to the intervention.

Both these projects work alongside the communities involved. Just as it is good practice to work 'in partnership' with families and young people when planning interventions, communities should be involved in deciding which risk factors should be investigated, what projects should be set up to reduce the risks and how outcomes should be monitored.

Most of the government initiatives now established around the country in disadvantaged communities such as Sure Start, Children's Fund/On Track and Connexions programmes are based on this model. Integral to all these programmes is some sort of evaluation at both a local and national level. As the evaluations come through, we may get a better idea of what programmes are effective, but the wide range of different projects used in different areas may make this difficult. It is important that from the beginning as many of the projects as possible only use programmes with proven effectiveness (Department for Education and Employment, 1999b).

The clinical audit

Another approach for assessing current practice in existing projects is the clinical audit:

> The clinical audit allows multi-disciplinary teams to actively and systematically review their practice with the aim of improving the quality of the services delivered and ultimately the outcomes for service users. (Hardman and Joughin, 1998)

The clinical audit, which should involve all stakeholders, has a number of stages that form an ongoing cycle. The stages include:

* *reviewing the literature* on evidence-based findings
* *setting standards* based on best practice
* *collecting data* on the current practice from all those involved, including clients

- *analysing findings*
- *changing practice*
- *reviewing standards and re-auditing.*

Audits may focus on a specific service provided for children and families or on specific aspects of a service, such as a course for anger management. Unlike research, an audit is usually led by the service providers, is an ongoing process and is specific to the service or project it is auditing. The process is helpfully described in a publication by the Royal College of Psychiatrists (Hardman and Joughin, 1998).

Generally speaking, the more complex the needs, the more aspects of the child's life should be investigated, the more agencies involved and the more time should be allocated for assessment. However, relatively straightforward cases have a way of becoming more complex.

There is considerable research evidence that the effectiveness of any intervention is linked to the specificity of the assessment. Assessments need to specify in clear, unambiguous terms the concerns, the child's or parent's needs, the family strengths and the goals of any intervention. To reach this stage there are some tried and tested tools.

Individual assessment tools

Many publications from the Department of Health such as the *Framework for the assessment of children in need and their families* (2000), *Working together to safeguard children* (1999) and all the associated material, now give very detailed guidance for assessing children in need, promoting their welfare and safeguarding children who may be at risk of 'significant harm'. Together with the *Framework for assessment of children in need* they are a useful pack of assessment tools which can guide practice. One of the most useful, as mentioned earlier, is the Goodman Strengths/Difficulties Questionnaire (SDQ) which comes in various formats for parents, teachers or children to complete (Goodman, 1997b).

General Health Questionnaire (GHQ)

This tool, to measure how well a person is coping with the stresses of living, is not in the Department of Health pack but can be purchased from NFER, Windsor (www.nfer-nelson.co.uk) for use by agencies and other professionals. It is a very simple measure that can be used to indicate parents who may need more support. In a study in Wiltshire (Buchanan et al, 2002) it was found that social workers were quite good at identifying children who had major emotional or behavioural difficulties but missed many parents who were depressed and in need of extra help.

Assessing the possibility of significant harm

In addition to the material from the Department of Health, experience dictates that the possibility of harm should always be considered even in relatively straightforward cases. The Victoria Climbie Inquiry (Laming et al, 2003) reminds us how things can go tragically wrong. The following simple risk analysis developed by Buchanan and used in practice over many years, has proved to be a useful framework for asking the important questions. Social work students on placement have found this checklist helpful. They recommend that it should be used as a mental checklist when working with *every* child, on *every* contact with the child or family. The checklist recognises that we cannot protect children from all risk. Indeed, there may be benefits for a child where a risk is taken. For example, keeping a difficult adolescent at home who is involved in very 'risky' behaviour may, in many cases, be safer than exposing him/her to the risks associated with public care.

An ecological assessment

Longitudinal research has given considerable support to 'ecological' interventions. The ecological assessment identifies parent/child/young person risks that can be reduced or protective factors that can be enhanced to provide 'compensatory' experiences.

What are the specific concerns?

What are the specific behaviours that cause concern?

Who do they effect? When? Where? How? What is the previous history?

What are the short-term effects on parent/child/others? Long-term effects?

Have I got the whole picture? Who else may know the family (see Climbie Inquiry)?

Present and past factors?	Present and past protective factors?
The potential losses from risk-taking?	The potential gains from risk-taking?
Factors that might increase risks?	Factors that might decrease risks?

The worst thing that could happen?

Figure 11 **A simple risk assessment**

The following example relates to a young girl. Lisa, age 12, was living in a very dis-advantaged family with four young brothers and sisters, an alcoholic father on benefit, and a mother with learning disabilities. Lisa was effectively caring for her younger brother and sisters but constant criticism from her father was undermining her confidence and her school work was suffering.

Person	Family	School/community	Wider world
Risks	Risks		Risks
• low self-esteem	• alcoholic father		• recession – high
• school work underachieving	• mother low ability		unemployment
Protective factors	Protective factors	Protective factors	
• good ability	• grandmother occasionally visits and is supportive	• strong music groups in school	
• good coping skills		• local community interest in youth musical group	
• musical talent			

Lisa's problems stemmed from her home life, but a number of agencies had tried to improve this and all efforts had failed. Her father would not get treatment for his drink problems and her mother refused help. There were no significant child protection concerns. Lisa's confidence, however, was helped and her resilience to cope with her difficult home life was increased by becoming part of the school band. The school band performed at various sites in the community and Lisa became something of a star as the drummer. Her progress was reported in the local newspapers. Her improved confidence was reflected in her school work. Her home life remained problematic.

An individual strengths/needs audit

The 'non-deficit' model or strengths/needs model of assessment originated from work with people with learning disabilities, where it was found that a focus on a person's strengths rather than their deficits led to more positive outcomes. In the strengths/needs model, 'problems' or risks are restated positively as 'needs'. In the hypothetical case below, John, age 14, has been involved in vandalism and petty crime with a gang of other boys from the neighbourhood. John's problems are stated *positively* as a need to find another activity to divert him from crime. His strengths are 'what he likes to do', 'what he has achieved in the past' and 'people or resources available to meet needs'. As can be seen, strengths are used to meet needs. The voluntary agency working in 'partnership' with his mother makes a financial contribution to John's training.

Strengths	Needs
John likes football and has some talent	John needs activity to keep him off the street and divert him from criminal activities
Uncle plays for local team	
Local team have training sessions for local youngsters for £1.00 per session	John's mum needs help to pay the cost of the training sessions
Voluntary agency has funds to subsidise sporting activities	
Uncle prepared to introduce John to local team and get him to initial training sessions	John needs someone to help him get to initial training sessions

The Looking After Children (LAC) materials

The Looking After Children Assessment and Action Records are now used in most local authorities in England and Wales. These schedules have been involved in a heavily researched developmental programme in the UK and elsewhere, and the indications are that, used correctly, the records assist in bringing about better outcomes for children (Ward, 1995). The schedules monitor seven key dimensions in a child's life: *health, education, identity, family and social relationships, social presentation, emotional and behavioural development* and *self-care skills*. Although these materials were developed for 'looked-after' children, they can also be used to assess and monitor other children coming to the attention of family support services.

The strength of LAC materials is that they improve practice by assessing the child's current situation and by focusing on action – what needs to be done. The records also provide useful information for managers. In a Canadian study, managers found that children in care were having considerable time off school for specialist appointments. As a result, action was taken to encourage rescheduling of appointments outside school hours.

The ABC assessment

The ABC assessment was originally a tool of behavioural psychologists and is the basis of many successful 'behavioural' programmes. The assessment involves identifying a clearly defined behaviour then noting what happened 'before' the behaviour (the antecedent) and then what happens 'after' the behaviour (the consequence). In the following example, Lisa is a 3-year-old girl with severe temper tantrums:

Antecedent	Behaviour	Consequence
When at the local shop Lisa asks for sweets.		
Mother says 'no'.	Lisa screams and screams. Everyone looks at her.	Mother buys Lisa sweets.

In this familiar scenario, it is easy to see that Lisa has developed a very effective strategy for getting sweets. She may take this 'learnt' behaviour into the home and screaming fits will be the order of the day whenever she is refused something she wants. Her mother too will have 'learnt' that to keep Lisa quiet it is quicker and easier to give her what she wants.

Antecedents may immediately precede behaviour or they may be a little more distant. Jimmy, age 8, always arrived at school in a highly agitated state and was unable to concentrate for the first half of the morning. The education welfare officer went to see his mother. She explained that the mornings were very stressful and they ended up screaming at each other. As the result of the assessment, a careful reward programme was set up involving both Jimmy and his mother. His mother would get things ready the night before (Jimmy would note on the chart that she had done this) and Jimmy would get himself together with the minimum of help in the morning (his mother would put a star on the chart to note that he had done this). A week later, a much calmer Jimmy was arriving at school.

Noting 'positive' behaviour rather than negative can also be helpful. Helen, age 4, was often very distressed in nursery for no obvious reason. Over several days staff kept a record of when she was not distressed. It became apparent that Helen was reacting to noise. The classroom was close to the road where there were some road works. She only became distressed when noise levels rose. As a result of the assessment, it was possible to move her to another class at the other end of school away from traffic noise and she became much calmer.

Figure 12 **Cognitive analysis and response**

Depression

Situation	Parent thinks (negative thoughts)	Parent responds	Child responds	Parent thinks (more negative thoughts)	Parent responds
Child makes living room into a mess	'I'm a terrible parent'	Criticism and spanking	More difficult behaviour	Mother feels more hopeless and helpless. 'It's all my fault'	Mother gives up trying to control child

Anger

Situation	Parent thinks (negative thoughts)	Parent responds	Parent responds as a result	Child responds	Parent further responds
Child makes living room into a mess	'He is impossible and lazy'	Emotions of anger. Physiological changes: blood pressure rises, etc	More yelling and criticism	More misbehaviour	More anger. More negative thoughts

Positive response

Situation	Parent thinks (positive thoughts)	Parent responds	Parent responds as a result	Child responds	Parent responds
Child makes living room into a mess	'I can cope – my job is to help him'	Decreased stress	Increasingly calmer and more rational response to child's behaviour	Decreased child misbehaviour	'I can cope without feeling hopeless or angry'

Cognitive behavioural assessment

Cognitive behavioural interventions are among the most successful for treating a range of problems in children and adults (Kendall et al, 1997; quoted in *Evidence Based Mental Health* 1998(2): p43, as an important example of the efficacy of cognitive behavioural therapy in children with anxiety disorders). In a cognitive behavioural assessment the central task is to help the person to identify and challenge the 'negative' thoughts (or cognitions) that get in the way of an effective response, and to replace them with 'positive' thoughts. The following examples are based on work by Carolyn Webster-Stratton. They are given here to illustrate the assessment method. Fuller details of the treatment for depression are given in Chapters 9 and 10. The Webster-Stratton child and parent training interventions (both behavioural and cognitive behavioural) have been extensively evaluated and have a robust track record (Webster-Stratton and Hammond, 1997).

Assessment of 'significant others'

Parents, friends, relatives and teachers can be important sources of good or ill. Young parents may be well supported by their own mothers, or the relationship can have devastating effects on their competence and confidence. Similarly, adolescents can have friends who are a positive influence or friends who lead them into trouble. Family therapists, who focus on family systems, often use *genograms* in therapy sessions to help them and the family understand the complex relationships and 'attachments' within the family group. Genograms are a drawing of a person's family tree. Front-line workers will also find that a genogram is a useful tool. Children and young people often enjoy the exercise of explaining 'who is who' in their family and drawing it out. During the process, many children reveal a vivid picture of their family life.

Another useful tool is an *ecogram*, which assesses relationships both inside and outside the family. An ecogram can be divided into informal supporters such as relatives and formal supporters such as GPs, teachers and doctors. The strength of the relationship is indicated by the strength of the line and the flow of the support by arrows. Destructive relationships can also be indicated.

Studies show that most people turn to their wider families at a time of need (see, for example, Buchanan and Ten Brinke, 1997a). This indicates both a *preference* for family help and an *expectation* that the family will be able to meet the need. Unfor-

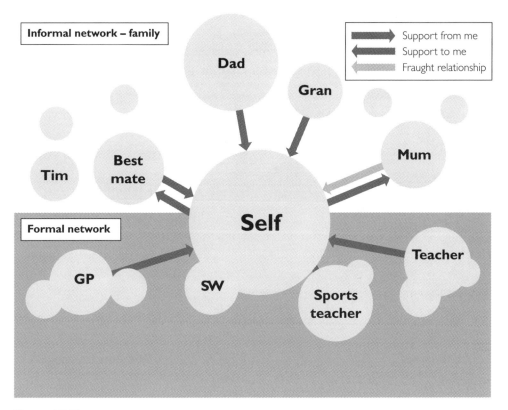

Figure 13 **Ecogram**

tunately, those who may need help most may have the families least able to give it. Social services and other agencies have an important role in helping the extended family to help.

Grandparents, for example, may be assisted to move closer to a single-parent daughter so that mutual support is more possible. Aunts and uncles may be inclined to have a turbulent nephew for the odd weekend to give his parents a break if funding is found to pay the costs of a visit. Family help is, of course, a two-edged sword. Some grandparents can be exceedingly helpful, but others can be exceedingly destructive. The ecogram helps sort out the different relationships.

Figure 14 **Motivational interviewing**

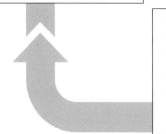

Pre-contemplation
Identify: assess, screen, enquire
Limit damage: health, relationships, education/employment
Motivate: feedback re. behaviour risks, situation, tolerance,
harms

Relapse
Minimise harm
Support, emphasise that lapse
need not be relapse, respond
to immediate problems
Re-engage
Assess point in cycle. Return
to task

Contemplation
Change motivation
Diary/inventory: monitor
effects of behaviour, elicit self-
motivating statements, affirm,
promote self-esteem, validate
ambivalence, reflect

THE CYCLE
OF CHANGE

Maintenance
Maintain behaviour change
Relapse prevention work,
work on other problems, alter-
natives to problem behaviour.
Support lifestyles change

Decision
Facilitate decision
Promote self-efficacy, envision.
Elicit requests for information.
Ask 'key questions'. Discuss
range of options. Negotiate
goals

Change
Change behaviour
Advice on problem behaviour
eg with alcohol abuse: limits,
cutting down. Detox, With-
drawal. Medical support, realistic time limited goals. Promote
self monitoring. Reinforce
gains

Assessing motivation to change

Very often the first step in helping parents, children and young people is to assess their motivation to change the behaviour that is causing them (or their children) distress/harm. The following technique has been widely used in probation, particularly with clients who have problem drinking and/or substance abuse.

'Motivational interviewing' is a well-proven strategic counselling approach. Central to motivational interviewing is the original Prochasta and DiClemente 'Cycle of Change' model (1982) (figure 14 is adapted from one used by James Sandham at the Department of Social Policy and Social Work at Oxford for use in probation training). This useful tool assesses the client's level of motivation and can be used with a variety of approaches. The model indicates tasks and interventions that are appropriate for the particular point in the 'change' cycle. The skill is to match tasks to the appropriate stage in the cycle of change. Motivational theory suggests that exploration of a person's ambivalence, avoidance of styles deemed to be road blocks, skilful use of reflective listening and the asking of evocative questions, can all be used to build motivation to change in what have previously been fixed behaviour patterns (Miller and Rollnick, 1981).

The model was originally developed for alcohol and substance abuse programmes but could be adapted for other types of cases. For example, in a family with four children aged 2–10, the children are totally out of control. The parents have used very punitive measures without success to try to discipline them. The children, who have come to the attention of social services, have been placed on the child protection register. Three months later things have not improved and the children are still receiving significant injuries as a result of being beaten. In the *pre-contemplation* stage the parents would consider with the social worker whether they wanted to change their way of relating to the children and to work on changing the children's behaviour; the *contemplation* stage may be looking more closely at what they are doing; the *decision* and then *change* stages will involve exploring how changes can be made and pursuing chosen strategies. *Maintenance* will be necessary as, when new stresses hit the family, *relapse* is a strong possibility.

Tools for talking to children and young people

Assessing the child's view of the world is central to effective intervention. Tools for communicating with children and young people are widely available. Both *Answers for carers: you and young people in your care* (Wheal and Buchanan, 1994, reprint 1999) and *The foster carers' handbook* (Wheal, 1995) are full of practical ideas for raising issues with children and young people.

Barnardo's also publishes a game called *All about me* (1995) for playing with children and young people. This follows the basic principles of board-games. Players roll a dice to progress around the board. If they land on a particular square they pick up a card. In this game all the cards are part sentences: 'I am very happy when ...'; 'I am very angry if ...'; 'My favourite colour is ...' This game has many uses. At a conference of contact centre workers, it was suggested as a useful way for non-resident parents to get to know a son or daughter they had not seen for some time.

More general questionnaires and checklists are included in the appendices of *Juveniles and children who sexually abuse* (Calder, 1997).

Key messages

- Reducing risk and enhancing protection requires both multi-agency and multi-level responses.
- It is crucial to any assessment to obtain a 'baseline' against which change can be measured.
- Professionals should become familiar with the various reliable and validated assessment tools.
- The well-being of the parent(s) should be considered as well as that of the child.
- Simple risk assessment should be undertaken.
- Negatives can be turned into positives with an individual strengths/needs audit.
- An ecogram can be helpful in working out who is a positive influence and who is not.
- Behavioural and cognitive-behavioural approaches to assessment should be considered.
- Motivational interviewing may provide a way of changing patterns of behaviour.
- Assessing the child's view of the world is central to effective intervention.

Part III
Interventions

7 Prevention projects

> Although mental disorders cost our nation billions each year in treatment, related support, and lost productivity, the funding for prevention of mental disorders has been inconsistent, due in some part to a lack of confidence regarding the effectiveness of specific programs. (Albee and Gullotta, 1997)

Very few 'prevention' projects have been systematically evaluated in the UK. It is important with the many initiatives to combat social exclusion in the UK, that projects should be based on programmes that have some evidence of effectiveness. In the US there has been a stronger tradition of systematic programme evaluation. Easily available lists of both 'successful' and 'promising' programmes can now be downloaded from the web (see Appendix I). These programmes often come with detailed instructions on how they should be implemented. Although the USA is different from the UK, by looking at some of these American studies we can elicit clues about what works and the mechanisms involved. In the UK, there are many innovative and exciting projects to promote children's well-being. Most of these have not been rigorously evaluated. In this chapter, a few of these UK projects are mentioned as examples of interventions that may work, because they incorporate some of the effective mechanisms identified in the US studies.

Targeted perinatal home visiting

In the UK, the **Social Support and Pregnancy Outcome** experimental programme (Oakley et al, 1990; Oakley, 1992) offered home visiting and 24-hour telephone support by experienced/specially trained midwives to pregnant women who had a history of low birth weight babies and social disadvantage. In the controlled study, average birth weight of babies compared to a control group was higher. There were fewer obstetric complications, mothers and babies were healthier and there was an increase in maternal well-being.

In another well-validated UK programme, health visitors, with additional training, delivered counselling and cognitive behavioural therapy to disadvantaged mothers who were experiencing depression following the birth of their child. At the

Table 3 **Perinatal home visiting**

Studies	Intervention	Outcomes	Why it works – possible mechanisms
Targeted home visiting for disadvantaged mothers prior to birth of child and through to 2 years. *Classic studies* Kitzman et al (1997); Olds et al (1997). These studies are urban replications of the earlier mainly rural studies.	1 Free transport to pre-natal care. 2 Developmental screening 3 Home visits by nurses • child development knowledge and skills/strategies • practical help for family problems • help to develop support networks	Considerable evidence that home visiting improves parenting and leads to positive outcomes for infants and young children. Parents less likely to abuse or neglect; homes more developmentally stimulating, less use of welfare. The earlier Olds et al studies show that 15 years later there is a reduction in subsequent pregnancies, substance abuse, offending and use of welfare.	The basic idea has been replicated in many studies. • Around birth of first child, mother is very willing to receive support and guidance. • Best programmes start before birth and continue up to 2 years. • More intense problems need more intensive interventions. • Interventions matched to needs of parent(s)/child more successful than standardised programmes.

18-month follow-up there were significant benefits in terms of maternal reports concerning the quality of the mother/infant relationship and reduced levels of behavioural disturbance in the toddlers (Cooper and Murray, 1997). An important element of the success was taking the intervention to the mother rather than expecting her to come to a clinic.

The researchers Cooper and Murray have developed a 17-item questionnaire, validated on a large population, that can be used at 32 weeks of pregnancy to identify around one in three of mothers at risk (Cooper et al, 1996). Since primary care workers are generally not well informed about postnatal depression, its causes, consequences and management, Murray and Cooper recommend that training is given in the use of their checklist.

Working with fathers

The evidence that fathers' involvement is protective against a range of life's adversities suggests more could be done to involve fathers. Work by Flouri and Buchanan (2003, 2002a,b,c)using data from the National Child Development Study (NCDS) shows very positive outcomes for children where fathers are involved. In this study 'father involvement' was indicated by fathers who took an interest in their children's education, who had an equal share with the mother in the management of the child and who went on outings with the children. Broadly speaking, children with involved fathers did better in school; boys were less likely to be delinquent; children's mental health was better; and, in the long term, the young people when they grew up had better relationships with their own partners. Fathers who were involved with their offspring before the age of 7 had happier relationships with them in adolescence.

The findings are strong but there are two important cautions. Related research is showing that where post-separation or divorced parents are in conflict over the arrangements for the children this may cancel out any benefit of non-resident father involvement at least in the short term (Welsh et al, forthcoming July 2004). Also, an important paper by Jaffee and colleagues (2003) shows that where fathers are seriously antisocial with major convictions, the more time they lived with their children the more conduct problems their children had. Children who did not live with their fathers with high levels of antisocial behaviour had fewer conduct problems. The findings did not hold for fathers who were only mildly antisocial.

Various projects around the country are now taking up the challenge of working with fathers. Much of current ongoing work with fathers is reported in the Fathers Direct web page (www.fathersdirect.com/). Fathers Direct, for example, report on recent research and run training courses for those working with fathers.

Table 4 **Working with fathers**

Studies	Intervention	Outcomes	Why it works – possible mechanisms
Fathers Plus – working with and for dads in Tyne and Wear has undertaken an audit of projects in the North East working with fathers (often unemployed) Key publication Richardson (1998)	• The Canny Lads • A dad's place • Dad's group • Work with Fathers • Chopwell Father's • Working with men All these groups except the last took place in family/neighbourhood centres and attracted small numbers of fathers with children. • Children/Fathers visit scheme HMP Durham Visits for children in chapel with toys.	Canny lads Group formally evaluated, but results not yet available. Fathers Plus audit of all the projects in the North East recommended a forum for group workers working with fathers is needed: to network, to support, to develop and to learn the best way of involving different types of fathers according to their different needs.	There is growing evidence that fathers' involvement especially with boys is important, but involving fathers is not straightforward. • Different groups for different fathers. • Different methods needed to engage different types of fathers. • Family centres may be too 'women' focused. • Fathers' work needs to be 'sold' to fathers. • Fathers' groups need men facilitators.

Pre-school programmes

The findings from the US **Headstart** and **Perry Pre-School** programmes have been very influential in the UK. The strong message from the Perry Pre-School study is that after 27 years there is $7 return for every $1 invested. Some suggest that the success of Perry Pre-School is due to its 'think-do-review' routine in the nursery school that teaches the children how to plan. This would link with Rutter's classic

Table 5 **Targeted pre-school programmes**

Studies	Intervention	Outcomes	Why it works – possible mechanisms
Classic studies eg Headstart (McKey et al, 1985) The High/Scope Perry Pre-School Study (Schweinhart and Weikart, 1993)	Key Elements *Headstart* Enjoyable active learning curricula, well-trained staff, good relationships between staff and parents, non-stigmatising.	*Headstart* In the long term, less use of remedial services, less offending, better school attainment, better track record in employment.	The *Headstart* programme was originally thought to have failed because gains in IQ were not sustained in primary school.
	Perry Pre-School The curriculum was based on a 'plan-do-review' routine. Task orientated. High levels of parent participation.	*Perry Pre-School* Fewer behavioural difficulties, lower drop-out rate, higher levels of educational attainment, lower teenage pregnancy rate, higher incomes and levels of home ownership.	The real pay-off from such programmes may only become apparent in the long term. The success of the High/Scope Perry Pre-school may be due to the 'plan-do-review' routine as well as the parent/school link.

study of institutionalised children that showed that those who had an ability to plan had much better outcomes as adults (Rutter and Quinton, 1984). Others feel that the success of the Perry Pre-School study is related to the parents' involvement and interest in their children's education.

Replications undertaken elsewhere show that programmes which engage children as active learners in an enjoyable process have better short- and long-term outcomes in emotional and behavioural terms as well as in attainment than those that do not engage the children. In Oxford, **PEEP** is an interesting example of an education-focused pre-school project that includes the whole catchment area of a secondary school, covering three highly disadvantaged areas. The project works in partnership with parents who are the child's first educators, using a structured curriculum:

> PEEP builds on the growing body of evidence which links such factors as the early development of language, literacy, personal and social development with outcomes relating to higher educational attainment, improved behaviour and crime prevention and the disposition to life-long learning. (PEEP, 1998)

Names of parents of new-born babies are obtained from the local maternity hospital. More than half of all eligible families take part. Provision is made for children aged 0–5. At each level there are different toys and books to borrow along with various ideas and suggestions for activities that can be done at home. There is a strong equal opportunities emphasis. Twenty-three languages are spoken by PEEP families. Translations are made of materials, diversity is valued (staff are representative of the ethnic and social mix of the community in which they work) and home visits are made to those who find attending groups difficult. Attendance patterns of the Asian families enrolled were comparable to the overall attendance of all families. Parents who have been in the programme have an opportunity to obtain accreditation for their learning under the Open College networks system. A major evaluation of PEEP's effects is due to be completed in 2005; an evaluation of the provision for 3–4 year-olds found that participating children made gains in language, number and self-esteem compared to non-participants (Evangelou and Sylva, 2001).

Sylva, who is closely involved with PEEP, has recenlty completed a five-year longitudinal study on the effects of different types of pre-school education (Sylva et al, 1999). Sylva concludes:

> If we were to make evidence-based decisions for preventing behavioural problems, we would recommend universal early childhood education. Educational practice should be shifted away from the current stress … on formal academic preparation towards the development of social skills and commitment … The most important impact of early education appears to include: children's aspirations, motivations and social adjustment. These are moulded through active learning experiences in the pre-school centre which enable children to enter school with a positive self-esteem and begin a career of commitment and social responsibility. (Sylva and Colman, 1998, p86)

Pre-school home visits with an educational focus
The following well-validated US project links with the ideas behind the UK PEEP programme.

Table 6 **Pre-school home visits with educational focus**

Studies	Intervention	Outcomes	Why it works – possible mechanisms
Parents as Teachers programme Central concept: Children are born to learn and children learn best from the people they love. It is community-targeted rather than family therefore is less stigmatising.	Home visits (one per month or more) by paid parent educator who gives information on child development and how to maximise everyday learning opportunities.	At the age of 3 children of participating families were advanced over the comparison group in language, social development, problem-solving and other intellectual abilities.	The success of this programme may be due to its focus on child development and education rather than social problems. The programme respects the diversity of parents and families while uniting them around a universal goal – raising healthy and successful children (Winter and McDonald, 1997).
Classic study Pfannenstiel and Seltzer (1985).	*Monthly group meetings* Special meetings for Dads.	A follow-up study of pilot project and comparison groups showed that in all behavioural areas participating children did better.	

Some of the characteristics of parents as teachers are seen in the promising **Wiltshire (UK) School Start** programme. This pre-school programme is targeted at children who may have difficulties in starting school. Vulnerable children (those with emotional or behavioural problems, speech difficulties, hearing problems, asthma and the like) are referred by health visitors and others to School Start. Before they start school, these children are visited by School Start Education Support Assistants (ESAs). Most of the ESAs are parents themselves, all have pre-school or nursery experience and all take a foundation course for non-professionals working with children before starting work. ESAs work with individual families using behavioural methods and focused play. They also undertake an extensive range of activities to support the families. The evaluation of the pilot study shows that the project has been very positively received by parents and schools. Schools report that the children involved have settled better into school than expected.

Also in the UK, Scott and Sylva (Sylva and Colman, 1998) have been involved in a randomised controlled trial comparing different interventions for 5-year-old children with behavioural problems. Sylva hypothesised that some children may need to settle their behaviour before they can develop the necessary skills to read. The Webster-Stratton materials together with a programme to involve parents in helping their children to read were used with one group of parents, while another group received standard services. Parents and children without behavioural problems formed a comparison group. The randomised controlled trial has demonstrated that children do indeed benefit from involvement in the programme.

Structured parenting group programmes

In an analysis of some 200 studies of primary prevention mental health programmes for children and adolescents, Durlak (1997b) found that programmes that relied exclusively on parent training were the only category that did not produce significant overall positive effects. He notes that programmes may need to be longer to produce an effect. He also notes the difficulty of recruiting parents for parent training. Smith, in reviewing parenting programmes in the UK, feels there are a number of unanswered questions about the effectiveness of parenting programmes although:

> Anecdotal evidence, parents' self-reporting and the views of a range of professionals all suggest positive outcomes for both parents and children in terms of a number of indicators. (Smith, 1998)

Webster-Stratton's programmes are well-validated. Their focus is on children who already have behavioural difficulties or 'conduct disorders'. Using her programmes based on behavioural and cognitive behavioural principles, about two thirds of these children will improve. These programmes, as written up in professional journals, can appear rather soulless and mechanistic. In the authors' experience, behavioural programmes do not work unless the child and parent are engaged in a way that stimulates their interest. A key component of the Webster-Stratton programmes is the

Table 7 **Parent training programmes**

Studies	Intervention	Outcomes	Why it works – possible mechanisms
A systematic review by Barlow (1997). *Classic studies* Patterson and Narrett (1990). Also studies by Webster-Stratton and Hancock (1998). Various studies are currently being undertaken in the UK using the Webster-Stratton videos and materials.	Broadly two types of programmes: relationship type and behavioural. Webster-Stratton programmes BASIC: 12-week, interactive play skills; reinforcement of positive behaviour; video-tape modelling, non-violent discipline. ADVANCED: plus depression, marital distress, poor coping skills, lack of support. SUPPORTING YOUR CHILD'S EDUCATION: how to strengthen children's education: home/school links.	Programmes based on cognitive/ behavioural principles have consistently been shown to be more effective than other types of programmes (Barlow, 1998; Webster-Stratton 1998). Studies by both Webster-Stratton and Patterson show that around 2/3 of families are helped. Replications of Webster-Stratton programmes in different areas in the USA have come up with similar results. Webster-Stratton notes that programmes have to be implemented in full to achieve expected results.	Barlow reviewed 255 studies of group-based parenting education and found only 18 where it was possible to assess effectiveness. Relationship-type programmes are harder to evaluate. Drop-out from parenting programmes can be high. Parents can feel stigmatised if access to the group is via 'parenting failure'. Programmes must 'engage' child and parent. Best programmes are fun.

'fun' way in which they involve the child and the non-threatening way they involve parents. The programmes also use a wide range of media to get the messages across, including videos and puppets. In 1998, in order to try to reach the last third of children who did not improve, Webster-Stratton introduced two new programmes: one to interact with mothers who are depressed and another to motivate parents around their child's education.

In the UK, parenting programmes are often run in family centres as part of a wider programme of activities. So far, research on the effectiveness of family centres is limited. This is partly because of the diversity of work and objectives sailing under the 'family centre' flag.

Howgill Family Centre in West Cumbria, for example, is based in Whitehaven but services are spread over a much wider area. Trained volunteers provide family support while the Howgill 'Hippopotabus', a well-equipped double-decker bus, is taken to communities that lack pre-school facilities. Another parent support group helps parents who are isolated by fears. In addition there is a pre-school group, carer and toddler sessions and equipment loan. Statistics show that large numbers of children and families who come through their services undertake a range of activities.

Smith, in a study of six family centres, found they had a variety of impacts on children and parents:

> Eight out of ten mothers felt their children had learned to mix and share, communicate, make friends, gain confidence and independence, and generally become more 'sociable'. Eight out of ten said they themselves had made friends. This is about sharing experience, reducing isolation, checking out problems, learning and sharing practical information, learning that it was 'normal' to have problems in bringing up young children, and building friendships that continued beyond the centre. (Smith, 1998)

The real benefit from family centres comes indirectly. In Smith's study, the family centres were all in areas of social disadvantage. Given the high levels of depression in mothers and feelings of isolation, in supporting mothers the centres played an important role in limiting the numbers of children with emotional and behavioural problems.

In Birmingham, a different approach has been taken with the **Wraparound** project. The project is of interest as it was a model for the Sure Start initiative. Pilot projects were undertaken in three primary schools where there was recently expanded part-time nursery education. The school then became the focus for integrated early years services for mothers and children: pre-school services, family support, pre-vocational training and wrap-around childcare. Among the services provided were information about availability of day care, community resources such as crèches, courses for mothers, drop-in days for parents to make contact with local adult training and advice services, individual sessions for parents plus a telephone hotline. Also included on some sites was a room for adult training and education to run alongside the nursery provision, as well as contact with health visitors.

Findings from the pilot studies concluded that although schools were an effective venue for parent services, a repeated message was that 'those parents most in need of support are the least likely, and the hardest to encourage, to come forward to receive it'. Outreach work either by health visitors or a voluntary organisation such as Home-Start is necessary to facilitate the home/school link. The project found that the younger the children the more motivated and willing the parents were to get involved. Generating interest in parent groups was often problematic but parents were more interested if there were facilities for the children such as playgroups, 'stay and play'.

Other interventions

Home visiting by volunteers
Home visiting programmes such as **Home-Start** use volunteers and are run by voluntary agencies. They fill the gap for those families who are unable or unwilling to take part in other services. Home-Start is only one example of the many excellent 'outreach' programmes being run in different areas.

Problem-solving in pre-school and primary years
Attachment theorists suggest that early relationships with parents and significant others are the prototype for later relationships. Buchanan and Ten Brinke (1997b) found that there were significant links between observing parental conflict in childhood, arguing with parents in adolescence and arguing with partner or spouse in adult life. This suggests that programmes to help children and young people develop the necessary skills to manage interpersonal conflict are likely to have long-term benefits. The following programme appears to confirm this.

In this chapter a strong emphasis has been given to early years programmes. This is

Table 8 **Pre-school outreach work**

Studies	Intervention	Outcomes	Why it works – possible mechanisms
Home-Start A UK voluntary organisation – trained volunteers offer regular support, friendship and practical help to young families under stress in their own homes, helping to prevent family crisis and breakdown (branches around the UK and in other countries),	Each scheme adopts the Home-Start standards and methods of practice and is managed by a multi-disciplinary committee and is supported by Home-Start UK.	Evaluation descriptive. Home-Start mostly valued by families – non-stigmatising but professionals were the filter. A complementary service rather than stand-alone. A flexible service.	Home-Start seems to answer the needs of families who cannot/ will not take part in other projects. Often families in transition following family break-up etc. 40% lone parents.
Evaluation Frost et al (1997)	*Tasks undertaken* listening, practical, budgeting, transport, supporting older children, play. Meeting social and educational needs of children and encouraging confidence in parenting.	Mothers report: improved emotional well-being; 55% felt improved informal network, 52% improved parenting (43% no sustained improvement).	Most Home-Start families face multi-problems and often ill-health. In 10% there are child protection concerns. May be more acceptable as non-statutory.

because the evidence suggests that it is easier to change a younger child's behaviour than that of an older child.

We need to remember that around 50 per cent of children who have problems at 7 will have come through them at 11, and similarly half of those who have problems at 11 will have 'recovered' by the time they are 16. There are therefore grounds for optimism that more can be done to increase these numbers. At present, however, there are far fewer well-validated programmes for older children.

Table 9 **Problem-solving in pre-school and primary years**

Studies	Intervention	Outcomes	Why it works – possible mechanisms
Interpersonal cognitive problem solving. Central concept: the quality of social relationships and capacity to cope with interpersonal problems are central to social adjustment.	*Teachers are trained* to teach the prepared curriculum to whole classes. The goal is, by using games, to help children develop empathy, ability to cope with frustration, and problem-solving skills.	*Nursery and kindergarten children* Teacher trained: study groups showed gains in problem-solving skills, peer acceptance, concern for others, initiative and significant decreases in teacher-rated acting-out behaviours.	1 These are 'whole' class programmes therefore no child is stigmatised. 2 The children are not only taught to recognise emotions but are also taught the skills to problem solve.
The initial programmes focused on children aged 4. When age-adapted the programme is viable for children age 9 to 12 *Classic study* Spivack, Platt and Shure (1976)	*A Parent Training* programme was developed for African American parents attending day care who did not receive the training at school.	When trained by mothers: improvement in problem-solving. Mothers also developed skills. Children less behavioural problems in school. Five-year follow-up treatment gains maintained. *Older children:* With older children treatment may take longer.	3 The main focus is on younger children who respond more quickly.

Table 10 **Social awareness and problem-solving in primary schools**

Studies	Intervention	Outcomes	Why it works – possible mechanisms
Central concept: 1 specific behaviours and cognitions reliably predict acceptance and rejection in the peer group 2 these skills can be enhanced through training and practice. Whole school approach *Classic paper* Elias and Clabby (1989)	*Teachers' curriculum includes* 1 skills linked with self-control, attending, turn-taking, impulse control, regulating emotions and communication 2 behaviours linked to peer acceptance 3 problem-solving/ decision-making skills 4 applying skills in changing social situations, eg, after-school clubs *Programmes for parents,* some using cable TV.	Pre and post intervention testing in two sites showed significant gains in inter-personal sensitivity, problem analysis, specificity of planning.	The findings appear to be less strong than some other studies. The outcomes may be due to problem-solving and learning how to plan.

Some of the characteristics of the above programme are seen in the **Oxford Family Links Nurturing Programme**. This programme is based on the work of Bavolek (1996) and was originally used for the prevention and treatment of child abuse and neglect. In Oxford, this whole school programme (2 hours per week for all 4–7-year-olds every term) uses cognitive (knowledge-based) and affective (feelings-based) activities to promote positive relationships between parents and children, to develop self-

Table 11 **Anti-bullying in school**

Studies	Intervention	Outcomes	Why it works – possible mechanisms
The classic study is that by Olweus (1993) in Norway.

Whole school policy. Goals: to reduce bullying; to establish an awareness of the problem; improve the social milieu of the school. | Establish firm limits of acceptable and unacceptable behaviour; monitoring and surveillance; consistent application of non-hostile and non-physical sanctions for rule restrictions; involving parents and teachers. | Longitudinal cohort design, eg, 11- and 12-year-olds, one year compared with 11- and 12-year-olds next year post intervention.

Whole classes that had implemented complete intervention associated with greater reduction in bullying. Parallel reductions in antisocial behaviour such as vandalism, theft and truanting reported. | The finding that reduction in bullying is associated with less antisocial behaviour shows that a school anti-bullying 'ethos' may directly influence levels of antisocial behaviour operating in the community. |

awareness and self-esteem and to teach children values. Parents are also offered a similar and parallel programme. This programme is currently being evaluated.

Anti-bullying programmes
Bullying is not only a concern for parents, as we saw in Chapter 4 but is a major worry and a cause of enormous distress for many young people in school. There have been a number of studies, and one of the best validated is the Bullying Prevention Program (Olweus et al, 1999).

'Bullying Prevention Program'

This programme has been identified as a model programme by Blueprints for Violence Prevention, part of the University of Colorado (Olweus et al, 1999). To qualify as a model programme, research must demonstrate that there is evidence of a deterrent effect with a strong research design, that the effect is sustained, with multiple site replication (in this instance, the USA, Norway, the UK and Germany).

The most comprehensive evaluation of the programme was carried out in Norway, using a sample of 2,500 elementary and junior high school pupils and a quasi-experimental research design. It found reductions of typically 50 per cent or more in the frequency with which they reported being bullied and bullying others. Evaluations of programmes in the USA (sample size 6,388), UK (16 primary and 7 secondary schools) and Germany (sample size 6,400) have produced more modest but still positive findings.

How it works

The programme is based on research suggesting that adult behaviour is key in the prevention of bullying. To this end, adults in the school, and to some extent at home, must become aware of the extent of bully/victim problems in their own schools, and must engage in changing the situation. This acknowledgement and a clear commitment by a majority of the staff to participate in the programme seems to be a key factor in its success. The programme consists of a school conference day to discuss bullying and plan interventions, the establishment of a committee to coordinate the school's programme, and increased supervision of students at bullying 'hot spots'. It also consists of the establishment of rules against bullying and regular class meetings with students as well as interventions with bullies and victims, and contact with parents of those involved using where necessary counsellors or school-based mental health professionals. The programme has been shown to result in:

- substantial reduction in boys' and girls' reports of bullying and victimisation
- a significant reduction in students' reports of general antisocial behaviour such as vandalism, fighting, theft and truancy
- significant improvements in the social climate of the class, as reflected in students' reports of improved order and discipline, more positive social relationships, and a more positive attitude towards school work and school.

Peer-led life skills teaching with adolescents

A strong theme runs through all of these programmes. First, that programmes are more successful at times of transition – new parents are more open to advice and help than established parents.

Here we see that young people on the edge of adolescence are more 'available' than older adolescents. The secret of effective interventions is not only getting the timing right, but also the approach. In early adolescence the key motivator is the peer relationship. The **GOAL** programme taps into this.

The **Northumberland Young People's Health Project** is rather different but shares some of the peer-led characteristics of GOAL. This project was funded by Northumberland health authority between July 1996 and July 1998 and has been further developed since (www.hda-online.org.uk). Projects are in many cases supported by young volunteers who are trained. This is seen as an opportunity for young people to develop effective and user-friendly models of healthcare,and to improve their access to the existing range of services that they can use without referral, including sexual health services.

The aims of the project are to develop young people's health sessions in seven towns across the county, to acknowledge young people's different needs and personal choices, and encourage their involvement as central to the developmental process.

Sessions are held outside conventional 'health' settings on a drop-in basis. Young people design the publicity materials and, in some areas, young people are employed as administrative/reception workers. Key staff are a youth worker, sexual health nurse, sexual health doctor and generic health worker. Key ingredients are felt to be the confidentiality statement; the rights and responsibilities of everyone at the session being clearly displayed; the supervision; the supported involvement of interested local young people; and the publicity material being designed by young people. The evaluation of the project was carried out by young people. A major achievement of the project was that men were able to access sessions (gender ratio: 51 per cent male and 49 per cent female). More than two thirds of those who attended once came back again and, unlike clinic care, attending in pairs or in groups was the norm. Most young people had heard of the project by word of mouth. Family planning was the main subject of inquiry. Perhaps most telling was the fall in conceptions to young women under 16 from a high (live birth and abortions) of 34 for the first 6 months of 1996 to a low of 10 for the first 6 months of 1998.

Table 12 **GOAL – a peer-led programme**

Studies	Intervention	Outcomes	Why it works – possible mechanisms
Going for the GOAL A peer-led programme for adolescents aged 10–15 on health-enhancing and health-compromising behaviours. Information and skills based. *Basic concept:* the future is important to youth. Those who do not have positive expectations are at high risk for health compromising behaviours. High-risk youth are not responsive to traditional health promotion programmes. Best teachers at this age are peers. *Manual:* Danish et al (1992)	Local skills centre staff trained community and school personnel (often college students) who co-ordinated programme and recruited high school student-leaders who were taught GOAL programme. After school two or three student leaders led 10 one-hour focus groups of up to 15 younger pupils Sessions included: *dare to dream; setting goals; making goals reachable; making a goal ladder; identifying and building your strengths; going for goal.*	A very well-validated programme. Findings show: participants recalled sessions; largely achieved goals compared to control group. Better school attendance: less reported increase in health-compromising behaviours, violence and problem behaviour. They thought the programme was fun. Useful and helpful for their friends.	1 peer-led and supervised by peers of peers 2 not preaching… focus on positive 3 starting in early adolescence.

Table 13 **Life Skills Training (LST) to prevent or reduce gateway drug use (tobacco, alcohol and marijuana)**

Studies	Intervention	Outcomes	Why it works – possible mechanisms
Life Skills Training One of the 'Blueprint model programmes', University of Colorado (Botvin et al, 1998). A three-year intervention implemented by teachers in schools beginning with the first year of secondary school. Costs approx £5 per student per year.	Consists of 15 sessions in the first year, 10 in the second and 5 in the third. Each session lasts about 45 minutes and can be given once a week or as an intensive mini-course. Students are taught 1) general management skills, 2) social skills and 3) information and skills specifically related to drug use.	Outcomes across 12 studies: tobacco, alcohol and marijuana use reduced by 50–70 per cent Long-term results at 6 years post intervention: • polydrug use cut by 66 per cent • pack-a-day smoking by 25 per cent • decreases the use of inhalents, narcotics and hallucinogens.	By teaching effective self-management and social skills the programme has the potential for reducing inter-personal motivations to use drugs and vulnerability to pro-drug social influences. Note that the young people are involved as soon as they enter secondary school.

Telephone/internet helplines

As we move into the new technologies, many of the following agencies are developing websites and interactive email advice lines. Appendix 2 gives a more comprehensive list of helplines and internet resources. Noted here are some of the better known.

- **Parentline** runs a helpline for parents with a freephone. This was originally run by the National Step Family Association but is available for all parents, not just step-parents. Parentline also publish many useful leaflets (De'Ath and Slater, 1992; Hylton, 1995). The work of **Childline** is well known, but other helplines also provide a useful service.

- The **Children's Legal Centre** is currently reorganising its services. Details can be found on clc.live.poptech.coop.

- **Young Minds** (www.youngminds.org.uk) runs a free national information service for parents, carers or professionals who are worried about the mental health or emotional well-being of a child or young person. Initial contacts are dealt with by trained 'front-line' staff, but parents who need detailed advice or consultation are offered a call back from one of Young Minds' team of 10 professional advisers.

  In 1997 an independent researcher evaluated the Young Minds service. Nearly half the calls related to young people between ages 12–17, peaking at 15 years. Of the 1,533 contacts, 95 per cent were by telephone and slightly more were about boys than girls. Depression, aggressive and disruptive behaviour, Attention Deficit Disorder (ADD) and hyperactivity were parents' most frequent causes of anxiety. More than half the callers reported that the call had made either 'a lot' or 'quite a lot' of difference to the way they saw the problems. Only 13 per cent said it had made no difference at all. More than 90 per cent also said that there had been definite advantages in having been able to contact the service by telephone. It was felt to be quicker and more accessible and many said they had found it easier to talk about the problem over the telephone than face-to-face.

- Better known are the **Samaritans** and their helpline staffed by volunteers who are available to listen in confidence on the telephone 24 hours a day, every day of the year. Because of the concern about increasing rates of suicidal behaviour in young people, the Samaritans have been publicising their work with young people. In 1999, Alison Weisselberg, Youth Co-ordinator for the Samaritans said:

  For many years the Samaritans have been visiting schools, youth clubs, further education colleges and universities. Our visits are an awareness exercise on several accounts: firstly to inform young people about the service we can offer; secondly to acknowledge the need of young people to be listened to and taken seriously; thirdly to encourage young people to turn to others and develop some life-skills themselves.

  The organisation's 200 centres are open for people to talk face to face as well. The national number (Tel: 08457 909090 (UK) and 1850 609090 (Republic of

Ireland)) can be contacted for the price of a local call. Young people can contact the Samaritans at jo@samaritans.org.

It was believed that correct information about drugs, sexuality, stress, for example, would motivate behavior change … Preventionists now recognise that systematic skill training is needed to develop prevention-related behaviors and mechanisms must be put in place to support and reinforce behavioral change after it occurs. (Durlak, 1997a)

Key messages

- The presentation of a project is crucial. Projects need to be non-stigmatising and meet the needs as seen by the parent/young person at the particular life-cycle stage.
- Projects that involve young parents in educational programmes to improve their child's start at school may have better outcomes than projects that try to improve their parenting skills.
- Some of the most needy parents will not/cannot go out to projects. They need to be seen at home.
- Fathers are important but we have a lot more to learn about how best to involve them.
- It may be easier to change a primary school child's behaviour than an adolescent's behaviour. It may be easier to change a child's or adolescent's behaviour than that of their parents.
- At different times parents, children and young people are more 'open' or 'closed' to interventions. Interventions at times of transition (eg, becoming a parent or becoming an adolescent) are usually more successful.
- Information is not enough. Parents, children and young people also need relevant strategies and skills. For children, learning to problem-solve and to plan and learning skills and strategies for managing social relationships are also important.
- For adolescents, peer-led programmes appear to have better outcomes.
- Telephone/internet helplines provide a useful service.

8 Children at special risk

The fact that aspirin relieves headaches does not suggest that an aspirin deficiency was the cause of the headache. (Robins, 1992)

The 19th century and early 20th century literature was replete with observations about the personalities of people who developed tuberculosis but the discovery of the organism and then of an effective antibiotic made such observations redundant. (Black and Cottrell, 1998)

This chapter considers approaches for children who because of their special situation may be at risk of psychological problems.

Children of substance-abusing parents

We know from research that children whose mothers abuse alcohol or drugs are vulnerable from the very earliest stages. Risk for these children starts before birth. After birth, because of their mothers' substance abuse during pregnancy, these childen may be particularly fractious and difficult to care for. As they grow, risk continues where the parent exposes the child either intentionally or unintentionally to opiates, stimulants, medication such as methadone, needles and so on. Children growing up in the homes of substance-abusing parents are at greater risk of poor parent/child interactions and emotional and behavioural disorders. Steps that can help troubled children include:

- working with parents during pregnancy to change them from being addicts first, mothers second, to mothers first, addicts second
- working with parents to reduce exposure to risk – looking at times of greatest use/withdrawal, security of drugs/needles
- increasing time-out for children, for example after-school clubs
- working with parents to improve parenting skills
- working with children to improve social and behavioural skills.

In the USA, the National Institute of Drug Abuse has identified the **Strengthening Families for the Children of Substance Abusing Parents** project as one that appears to be effective.

Table 14 **Strengthening families of substance-abusing parents**

Studies	Intervention	Outcomes	Why it works – possible mechanisms
***The Strengthening Families Programme (Kumpfer, 1987) A family-focused selective prevention programme for 6–10-year-old children of substance abusers.	14 consecutive weekly sessions, which last 2–3 hours. Optimal size 6–8 parents and 6–7 children. *Parent training* focus: parenting skills and reduction of parents' substance abuse. *Children's skills* focus: discussion of negative behaviours and development.	Evaluation suggests the programme is effective in enhancing family relationships, reducing family conflict, improving communication and organisation, and in improving the behaviour of children by reducing conduct disorders, aggression, and emotional problems. Positive results from over 15 independent research replications demonstrate that the programme is robust and effective. SFP has been modified for African American, Asian/Pacific Islander, Hispanic and American Indian families, rural families, and families with early teens. Canadian and Australian versions have also been tested.	The key to the success may be the focus on the whole family as well as the focus on the wider issues.

Table 15 **The Wonders model and the 'Difference Game'**

Studies	Intervention	Outcomes	Why it works – possible mechanisms
**The Wonders Model* (Fitzgerald and Mlinarcik, 2001) Serves women of childbearing age who used substances during pregnancy, their children up to the age of 14, adoptive/foster parents and other caregivers. Transport provided to the site. It is staffed by nurses qualified in infant massage, an occupational therapist, a family therapist, and two others.	The programme consists of five classes and involves *The Difference Game*. (This has been one of the most effective instruments used by case managers in the Seattle Birth to Three Advocacy Project for high-risk alcohol and drug abusing mothers. See, for example, Grant et al, 1997.) Each card begins with the phrase, 'It would make a difference in my life if I had …' and ends with a phrase such as 'a better relationship', and so on. A therapist plays the game with each parent and discusses ways to meet goals.	Descriptive data showing good outcomes for the Wonders Model but as yet no randomised controlled trials. Good evidence that the Difference Game is a very effective tool for working with this group.	The Difference Game encourages parents to make their own choices rather than have them imposed by professionals.

In the UK, help for substance abusing parents and their children tends to be either treatment or family support (social services) led. Again, the US may be leading the way in providing a programme that can be initiated with the child's birth where there is evidence of prenatal substance abuse.

In the UK, a **Drug Liaison Midwife Service** (www.worcestershire-smat.org.uk/ services/preg/asp) has been set up within the Worcester area. Two midwives noticed that pregnant women were often not reporting their drug use to them through fear of initiating social services' involvement and perhaps losing their children to care. Realising the risk from drug use to both mother and unborn child, they set up the Drug Liaison Midwife Service. To date they have successfully introduced themselves and their aims to a network of professionals, gaining enthusiasm and encouragement from all areas, to continue this project. It is a much needed project due to the increasing level of drug use within the young, reproductive age group. The multidisciplinary team includes obstetricians, paediatricians, midwives, health visitors, social workers, drug agencies, GPs, virologists, HIV experts, family planning experts, pharmacists and alcohol abuse agencies.

Children experiencing divorce

Although most children do not experience long-term psychological problems following divorce, a minority do. Around family breakdown almost all children experience some distress which may interfere with their school work and affect their social relationships. The worst outcomes are likely to be where the break-up is surrounded by conflict (Buchanan et al, 2001). The following school-based preventive mental health programme has been well validated in the USA on different populations and in different areas.

Projects for supporting children going through family break-up are developing in the UK. In Oxford, for example, the **Oxford Family Mediation Service** (125 London Road, OX3 9HZ; tel 01865 741871 or email mediate@ofms.fsnet.co.uk; nationwide contact numbers may be accessed via the website www.nfm.u-net.com/a-z.htm) runs a support service for children and young people going through parental separation and divorce.

Table 16 **Children of Divorce Intervention Program**

Studies	Intervention	Outcomes	Why it works – possible mechanisms
Programmes from kindergarten through adolescence. Aim: to create a supportive group environment where children can share experiences, clarify misconceptions and develop skills to cope with changes. Original paper: Pedro-Caroll and Cowen (1985)	Scheduled in school to ensure safe environment Programme geared to needs of each age group: eg young children: sadness, confusion, guilt, fear of abandonment; aged 9–12: loyalty, conflicts, anger isolation; young adolescents: promoting trust in future relationships. Also age-appropriate setting and method.	Evaluated extensively on different populations and ages. Programme children when compared to matched controls show significant improvement in behaviour and competence. Parents reported better home adjustment, communication, reduction in divorce-related concerns. On follow-up improvements maintained also children more positive about futures.	The programme could be modified for children experiencing multiple stresses including family breakdown. The success of the programmes may be related to matching the different needs of children at different ages, giving children an opportunity to express emotions safely and teaching them strategies and skills to cope.

Living with domestic violence

Exposure to hostility and discord between parents is an important determinant of emotional and behavioural problems in children of all ages, especially if the discord is persistent over time and the child becomes embroiled in hostilities between the parents. Family violence can take many forms and does not necessarily involve physical assault. (Falkov, 1998)

Even when domestic violence is suspected, the violence may not be mentioned. It is necessary to ask both the parent and the child: 'Have you ever been frightened by …?'

Many women do not identify with prevailing images of 'battered women' and thus do not see what is happening to them as 'violence' (Hester et al, 1996). Fears about social workers 'taking children away' can deter mothers from seeking help. Hester and Radford found that:

The greater their (professionals') knowledge of women's experiences of violence from male partners, and the impact of such violence on the women concerned, the safer and more positive their outcomes were likely to be for both women and children. (Hester et al, 1996, p4)

In a further study comparing practice in the UK and in Denmark which involved interviewing women survivors and associated professionals, Hester and Radford (1996) made the following recommendations in relation to practice. One of their key findings was that domestic violence often continued after the separation, and that women and children who had been victims of domestic violence could be placed at risk when the divorce court recommended contact with the non-resident parent.

- Professionals need to have a thorough understanding of domestic violence 'including the many forms that abuse perpetrators use, the continuation of violence after women leave, and the impact which domestic violence may have upon the safety and welfare of both women and children'.
- Those working with domestic violence need to recognise the link between the safety of mothers and the welfare of children.
- There is a need to take women's accounts of domestic violence seriously and to create an environment which is safe for disclosure.
- The importance attached to maintaining children's contact with fathers can, in some circumstances, undermine the welfare of individual children.
- There is a need to recognise the harm done by forcing agreement, mediating or conciliating when there is a history of domestic violence.
- There is a need to ensure safety at a time when women are most at risk of domestic violence.

- There is a need to ensure culturally appropriate places of safety. At present a disproportionate number of women from ethnic minorities are in refuges, yet few cater for specific cultural or religious groups.

The Family Law Act 1996 provides for occupation and non-molestation orders, which may be applied for through the civil courts. Many women, however, may find taking the initial step difficult. Women's Aid (www.womensaid.org.uk) suggests that support should be given as follows.

- Approach the woman in a non-blaming way. Explain to her that she is not alone and that there are many women like her in the same situation.
- Acknowledge that it takes strength to trust someone enough to talk to them about experiencing abuse. Give her time to talk. Don't push her to go into too much detail if she doesn't want to.
- Acknowledge that she is in a scary, difficult situation. Tell her that no-one deserves to be threatened or beaten, despite what her abuser has told her. Nothing she can do or say can justify the abuser's behaviour.
- Support her as a friend. Be a good listener. Encourage her to express her hurt and anger. Allow her to make her own decisions, even if it means she isn't ready to leave the relationship. This is her decision.
- Ask if she has suffered physical harm. Offer to go with her to the hospital if she needs to go. Help her to report the assault to the police if she chooses to do so.
- Be ready to provide information on the help available to abused women and their children. Explore the available options with her. Go with her to visit a solicitor if she is ready to take this step.
- Plan safe strategies for leaving an abusive relationship. Let her create the boundaries of what is safe and what is not safe; don't encourage her to follow any strategies that she is expressing doubt about.

Look after yourself while you are supporting someone through such a difficult and emotional time. Ensure that you do not put yourself into a dangerous situation; for example, do not offer to talk to the abuser about your friend or let yourself be seen by the abuser as a threat to their relationship.

*Norfolk Park Community Groups/Organisations: Sheaf Domestic Violence Project (DVP)

The Sheaf Domestic Violence Project (DVP) provides support to those suffering from domestic violence and works to raise awareness of the problem.

The project was established in 1996 and works directly with women, children and men who have been or still are suffering from domestic violence.

The organisation offers face-to-face visits, an escort service to court/hospital etc. It also co-ordinates the activities of other relevant agencies in the area.

The DVP also facilitates self-help groups and provides training or 'hands on' workers and volunteers to enable them to recognise the signs of possible domestic violence and respond appropriately.

Contact
67 Walden Road
Sheffield
S2 3PJ
Tel: 0114 249 8881 or 249 8882

Some people may prefer to talk in confidence. Helplines such as the Women's Aid National Domestic Violence Helpline (0800 2000 247) or the Refuge 24-hour Crisis Line (0870 599 5443) can offer advice and support.

Government recognition of the importance of domestic violence is set out in their guidance, *Domestic violence: break the chain* (Home Office, 2000b) which provides examples of good practice.

*Newham monitoring system

As part of the Newham Domestic Violence Strategy, Newham Domestic Violence Forum has set up a central monitoring system for domestic violence. This provides information about the levels of domestic violence in the borough and tracks the numbers of contacts different women are making with the various services. It aims to prevent the double counting of women who contact more than one service and to identify gaps in provision.

Contact
Newham Council Social Services Department
Gable House
27a Romford Road
Stratford
London
E15 4LL
Tel: 020 8430 2000 ext 30135 or 30136
www.newhamdvf.org.uk

Supporting young carers

The Department of Health (1995b) defines a young carer as:

> A child or young person (under the age of 18) who is carrying out significant caring tasks and assuming a level of responsibility for another person which would usually be taken by an adult.

Local authorities have duties and powers to help young carers and their families under the Carers (Recognition and Services) Act 1995, the Children Act 1989 under the 'children in need' provision, the NHS and Community Care Act 1990 and the Carers and Disabled Children Act 2000. Some children take pride in their caring responsibilities but others find the consequences of caring can lead to problems such as poor school results; poor concentration and bullying; isolation from peers; conflict, guilt and resentment; feeling left out of the decision-making processes; and lost opportunities. A major problem is identifying young carers who fear that social service intervention will lead to family break-up and separation. According to research (Dearden et al, 1998; Frank, 1995), young carers want:

- to be able to talk about their difficulties; someone to talk to
- to have recognition for their role
- opportunities for normal activities
- to achieve full potential
- support at school if necessary
- to be able to share the care responsibilities (domestic and practical help)
- to be involved in the decision-making process; to have information and prognosis
- a contact person in the event of a crisis.

Projects for young carers have sprung up around the county. Many of these are run by voluntary agencies and involve young people in group leisure activities.

KEY STUDY

Family group conferences

In Hampshire, the **Children's Society** has set up an interesting project using family group conferences to involve children and their families in the decision-making process at critical times. The purpose is to increase young carers' participation in the decision-making process. The Children's Society's project for young carers is being evaluated.

The possibility of using family group conferences with young carers is new. Family group conferences have, however, been widely used in the decision-making process with families where children are involved in child protection, youth justice or are at risk of being accommodated. In Wiltshire, systematic use of family group conferences as a substitute for conventional child protection conferences is being researched.

Family group conferences originated in New Zealand where it is mandatory for all children going through child protection proceedings to be the subject of such a conference (Marsh and Crow, 1998). Basically the model involves the wider family being brought together, being told about the child welfare concerns, and being asked to make a plan (in the privacy of their family group meeting) to ensure the well-being of the child/children involved. In the UK, social services usually offer some help in terms of resources.

Children living with parental mental illness

Between 5 and 7 million adults are suffering from a mental illness at any one time and 30 per cent of these will have dependent children (0–18 years old). Around 10,000 children and young people have caring responsibilities for parents with mental health, alcohol and/or substance abuse problems. Between a third and two thirds of these children will be adversely affected (Falkov, 1998).

Although some parents with mental health problems can care adequately for their children, all such children are at risk of emotional and behavioural problems and some are at risk of significant harm. Young children living with a depressed primary carer may miss the vital stimulation so necessary for healthy development in the early years. A toddler living with an under-active depressed mother may become over-active to attract her attention. Older children may have their childhood disrupted when their sick parent goes in and out of hospital. Other children may be directly at risk when they are involved in their parent's psychotic hallucinations.

A training pack and reader developed by the Department of Health, *Crossing bridges* (Falkov, 1998) explores this complex area. The challenge for all those working with mentally ill parents is to see the family holistically and 'cross the inter-agency/inter client-group bridge'. This publication outlines the evidence: the impacts of mental health problems on children and parents; the legal and policy frameworks; system and organisation frameworks; and recommended interagency responses. It suggests that practitioners should adopt the following approaches.

- Be realistic and honest in discussion with parents about their children. Give information about who is looking after children and how they are coping. Make practical plans about communication and contact with children, according to circumstances and safety. Consider what explanation is given to the children.
- Prepare children and their parents for admission to hospital whenever possible. Plan how to maintain links with the family during hospitalisation.

- Ensure that the first 24 hours of a person's admission to hospital are as positive as possible.
- Maintain links with family and children during hospitalisation. The service user is also a mother, an employee, someone who has to pay bills and someone who has important relationships.

In the same publication (here adapted from Heide Lloyd, in Falkov, 1998) a mother who had mental health problems writes of the needs of her children.

- It is imperative that children have as much access to information about the mental health of a parent as they are able to cope with.
- They should be free to discuss their feelings and ask any questions they wish to ask whenever they wish to do so.
- The simplest of things such as their normal diet, daily routine and contact with friends/family must be taken into account.
- Their moods should be understood and not just reacted to.
- During the worst part of a parent's illness, when perhaps the child will not be able to have contact with that parent, they should be continually reassured and have access to an individual they can confide in and trust with their fears, such as: Will their parent die? Will they ever live together again? Will they be like that when they are grown up?

KEY STUDY

*Meeting all the family's needs when a parent is mentally ill

The Family Welfare Association's **Building Bridges** services (www.fwa.org.uk/innovation.html) help families where a parent suffers significant mental ill-health. To support each family member means it has to fill the gaps between mental health and children's services. While health service professionals give therapeutic help to the parent, FWA will bring in children's services to help resulting problems caused to children. FWA can provide day-to-day support in the home to ensure all the family's needs are met. The result of this intense therapy and practical assistance helps to keep children at home and parents out of hospital.

Another related service run by FWA is its **WellFamily** service, providing a social care service for doctors' surgeries. Co-ordinators work with health service professionals who refer patients with practical and emotional issues which are making them ill.

A particular strength of much of the work undertaken by FWA are its services for minority groups and refugees and asylum seekers. Mainstream services often struggle to meet the needs of these groups, in particular their mental health needs. In Tower Hamlets, for example, many of the FWA service users are members of minority groups whose previous lives have left them too frightened to leave home. FWA workers visit them in their own homes so that they can use mainstream services such as schools and healthcare and begin to rebuild their lives.

Runaways

(A runaway is defined as) a young person aged under 18 who has left home or local authority care without agreement and has stayed away for a 'significant period of time', the length of time regarded as significant being related to the age of the runaway. ... a runaway is not the same as a 'young homeless person'. ... the essence of the term 'runaway' is that she or he is away without consent. (Abrahams and Mungall, 1992)

In 2002 the Social Exclusion Unit reported the following facts about runaways.

- Each year, 77,000 young people run away, including 20,000 children under the age of 11.
- The vast majority of these young people (80 per cent) do so because of family problems.
- They are five times more likely than their peers to have problems with drugs.
- They are seven times more likely than their peers to have been physically abused.
- Running away can lead to social exclusion, including homelessness, crime, prostitution and drug taking.

However, children in care are also at risk.

- Those in residential care are more likely to run away than those in foster care.

- Ten per cent are regular truants from school.
- Twenty-five per cent of the reported runaways had previous criminal convictions.
- Seventy-eight per cent of runaways from care came into care under a court order.
- Twenty-one per cent came into care under a voluntary arrangement.

Reasons for running away from home:

- arguments
- being 'grounded'
- gender differences: different rules for boys and girls
- deep-seated conflicts between parents and children
- to avoid difficult encounters, eg, court cases
- theft from home
- serious emotional crisis – at risk to themselves and others
- the experience of abuse.

Reasons for running away from residential care:

- absence of explanations
- way home is run
- group dynamic of the home – bullying
- unsuitable residential care placements
- residential placements away from home areas
- abuse in care.

KEY MESSAGES FROM YOUNG PEOPLE IN CARE

Barnardo's (1998) asked young people in care what might have prevented them from running away. They suggested:

- having someone to talk to who will listen
- responding to individual needs
- respecting confidentiality
- a safe place out of school
- information to be provided in schools
- information provided outside schools to be made available in a public place.

Young people confirmed that running away was more likely to happen when there was a breakdown of trust in social workers. They felt they needed more help throughout their care experience to reduce their vulnerability to running away and support on a one-to-one basis with someone already known to them.

Checkpoint is a drop-in centre based in Torquay, providing services for children and young people aged 13–25. It aims to promote and safeguard the well-being of children and young people at risk of social exclusion. The centre provides young people with advice, support and services, as well as undertaking outreach work.

Checkpoint is based on a 'hub and spoke' model that allows young people to access specialist services such as the South Coast Runaways Initiative in a friendly way through a central drop-in centre. The range of services is shown in the diagram below:

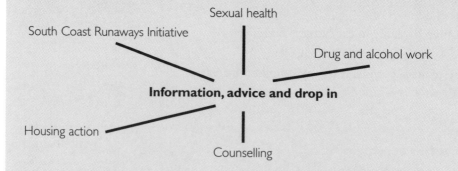

Checkpoint saw 913 named individuals in 2000/01. Of the 48 that the South Coast Runaways Initiative saw, 19 returned home, 2 were accommodated by the local authority, 14 were placed with their extended family, 3 remained runaways, and the status of 6 was unknown.

Figure 15 **South Coast Runaways Initiative, Checkpoint, Torquay (adapted from Social Exclusion Unit, 2002)**

An example of good practice from the US

In the US a more comprehensive telephone helpline service for runaways has been developed.

THE NATIONAL RUNAWAYS SWITCHBOARD (NRS), USA (WWW.NRSCRISISLINE.ORG)

This is a federally funded national communications system that aims to facilitate:

- a 24-hour confidential free helpline providing solution-focused crisis intervention
- referrals to community-based organisations across the country using an on-line database to more than 16,000 youth-related agencies
- three-way calling and mediating between young people, parents and agency staff
- a link to the Home Free transport service
- a message help service
- a prevention and education strand featuring information and publicity materials on running away and youth homelessness.

The helpline receives over 2,000 calls a week: 57 per cent of callers are runaways; 26 per cent are young people in crisis; 11 per cent are thinking about running away; 4 per cent are runaways thrown out of home; 2 per cent are homeless.

NRS makes extensive use of radio public service announcements to advertise its services. Television public service announcements are expensive but NRS is currently developing its strategy.

Children at risk of suspension from school

Finding appropriate and effective educational provision for the increasing numbers of children suspended from school is a major challenge. Front-line workers know that it is only a matter of time before a child suspended from school gets into more serious difficulties.

In October 1997 the government Green Paper, *Excellence for all children – meeting special educational needs* (Department for Education and Employment, 1997), outlined eight principles. Among these were working with parents; a framework for provision – based on Special Educational Needs (SEN) Code of Practice; increasing inclusion – support for SEN children in mainstream schools; and planning for children with emotional and behavioural difficulties (EBD).

A study from the Department for Education and Employment (Daniels et al, 1998) examined mainstream schools' responses to pupils whose special educational needs result from emotional and behavioural difficulties (EBD). The aim was to identify how mainstream schools achieved effective practice in the assessment, provision and evaluation of practice for pupils with EBD. The study noted that the characteristics of effective practice were good teaching; an appropriate curriculum; an effective behaviour policy; effective leadership; a core of dedicated staff; staff who are able to learn from their actions; and key members of staff who understood the nature of emotional and behavioural difficulties. Among the key themes for effective practice were creating and maintaining a positive school environment – the caring school, the talking school, the learning school; and appropriate behavioural policy for pupils with EBD – inclusive values, respect and specific management approaches.

The report from the Social Exclusion Unit (1998) describes truancy and school exclusion or school difficulties as 'a joined-up problem' requiring 'joined-up solutions'.

A survey of social service departments (Vernon and Sinclair, 1998) shows that joint projects between social services and education departments are developing, but to date few projects have been evaluated and there is no firm evidence on effectiveness. These newer projects:

- have a preventive focus – they aim to maintain children in school, rather than to reintegrate them
- target the younger child – those in the early years of secondary, primary and even pre-school
- provide support to the child and family and encourage new ways of supporting and liaising with schools.

Why are children excluded?
As the following table shows, the vast majority of children are excluded for behavioural problems rather than for what might be termed 'criminal offences' such as physical abuse and assaults on staff, arson or vandalism (Social Exclusion Unit, 1998).

- Bullying, fighting and assaults on peers   30%
- Disruption, misconduct and unacceptable behaviour   17%
- Verbal abuse to peers   15%
- Verbal abuse to staff   12%
- Miscellaneous   8%
- Theft   6%
- Defiance and disobedience   5%
- Drugs (smoking, alcohol, cannabis)   4%
- Vandalism and arson   2%
- Physical abuse and assault on staff   1%

There is also some evidence to suggest that competition in schools' performance tables may be partly to blame for the rise in the number of exclusions.

Who is excluded?

Although information on 'fixed-term' exclusions of between 5 and 15 days is not collated, OFSTED estimates that each year there are about 100,000 such exclusions of which a proportion will involve repeat 'offenders'. Perhaps more worryingly, the number of permanent exclusions rose from 4,000 in 1991–92 to about 13,500 in 1996–97, and of those permanently excluded, only about one third are reintegrated (Social Exclusion Unit, 1998). These figures, however, have fallen more recently.

- Eighty-three per cent of excluded children are boys and 80 per cent are aged 12–15.
- African-Caribbean children are six times more likely to be excluded.
- Children with special needs are more than six times more likely to be excluded.
- Children in care are more than 10 times more likely to be excluded.

What can be done?

Children are largely excluded for behavioural problems. Broadly, research suggests that harsh, authoritarian and neglectful parenting is strongly linked to conduct disorder in boys and internalising/emotional problems in girls. The very high percentage of boys at risk of exclusion suggests that information and programmes based on positive parenting strategies directed at both parents and early years staff are needed from the early years in order to prevent later behavioural problems.

The evidence so far suggests that the disproportionate number of African-Caribbean children being excluded relates not so much to disproportionately high levels of behavioural disturbance as to difficulties in teacher/child interaction. With this in mind, the Department for Education and Skills is currently considering how to attract more African-Caribbean teachers and learning assistants into schools.

What works to limit exclusion?

- Some children can avoid full exclusion by being kept in school through 'internal exclusion' from, for example, part of the school or a particular lesson. It ensures children are on site all day, learning, rather than roaming the streets. Some schools have 'sanctuary' rooms where children can be sent to cool off, under supervision, for a lesson or two.
- Dual registration at school and a Pupil Referral Unit (PRU) can mean the child gets specialist support without having to be excluded from the school. It can help if the PRU is on the same site as the school.
- Learning mentors can play a key role in supporting children at risk of social exclusion.
- If groups of schools work together to run informal 'one in–one out' arrangements for excluded children, time out of school is minimised.
- When a child already has special educational needs, it is generally better to hold a review to find alternative or additional resources rather than to exclude.

KEY STUDY

Examples of projects that reduce exclusion (Social Exclusion Unit, 1998)

The London Borough of Newham has succeeded in reducing the numbers of children excluded from school, including black and other minority ethnic children, children in care and children with special educational needs. Its policies have been agreed corporately by the council. The numbers of permanently excluded children have decreased across the authority in secondary schools from 76 in 1993–94 to 31 in 1996–97.

Langdon School, East Ham is a large comprehensive in which did not exclude any pupils in 1996–97 and only one pupil in 1995–96. It has a whole-school approach that includes:

- very clear preventive policies
- home-school agreements
- targets for each pupil
- a sanctuary room for children.

KWESI is another successful, rapidly growing project in Birmingham. It was started after concern about high exclusion rates and low attainment of African-Caribbean children. KWESI largely provides mentoring support to schools. The project has won the support of both schools and the local education authority, has successfully recruited from the community, trained and put in place mentors and has seen exclusion rates falling by 23 per cent. Two thirds of this reduction are ethnic minority pupils.

What may help the child who cannot be reintegrated? (Social Exclusion Unit, 1998)
Those who are not reintegrated may receive tuition at home for a few hours a week, or in a college of further education. The child who has not been reintegrated needs the following.

- *Consistency and support.* Home tuition needs to be provided quickly, on a regular basis, with consistent support/praise/discipline from the co-worker.
- *Time spent out of the home.* Educating excluded children may also include trips to museums, parks and so on, which can give the parent 'time off' and allow the child to socialise within a context of proactive learning.
- *Work experience.* Some older children who have already missed out on large parts of their education may benefit from work experience or a weekend job, and the chance to be treated as an adult.
- *Skills building.* Building on the child's strengths gives them confidence in their abilities.
- *Structure.* Home tuition for a few hours a day often leaves a child to roam the streets, or to spend endless hours in front of a television. Where school is not an option, an alternative daily structure should be found.
- *A future.* Excluded children want to plan for a realistic future just as those in school do. Children should be encouraged to look at the options, and to explore what they would have to do to achieve them.

WHAT HELPED SAM?

Sam was permanently excluded from school and living in a children's home after his dad died and his mum left him. With severe behavioural problems, his home tutor and key worker frequently changed. A new home tutor experienced in children with similar problems was engaged. By providing material that engaged his attention, ignoring attention-seeking behaviour, and praising achievements however small, a bond was slowly established. Excursions to parks and museums established that Sam was good at map reading, and loved to direct the tutor's route, so giving him a sense of pride and responsibility. Sam is now back in school for a few hours a week supported by his home tutor. Good communication between the home tutor, social services and the school has helped to support him. She has also found him a small job in the school canteen, so that he can learn in an active environment. Sam is not out of the woods yet, but consistent support and encouragement is beginning to pay off.

KEY STUDY

Example of good practice at local authority level (Social Exclusion Unit, 1998)

Include (previously called Cities in Schools) works in partnership with 25 local authorities to help over 1,000 young people who are all either excluded or long-term non-attenders; 40 per cent are persistent or serious offenders and 33 per cent are in care. Include's Bridge Courses for 14–16-year-olds who have suffered irretrievable breakdown in their education blend a further education course with work experience and a personal development programme supported by a key worker. The full-time cost is about £5,000, which compares to an average of £8,000 for education otherwise (education otherwise meaning not educated in school, eg, home tuition). Include is also developing reintegration and prevention services.

Key messages

- Prevention is easier than protection.
- Parents and their children need help to manage change.
- Needs must be identified and protective factors strengthened.
- There are programmes that can help children at special risk.
- Young carers are a special group and need to be recognised.
- Young people want someone to listen to them, and to respect their views.

9 Managing emotional and behavioural problems in children age 3–10

> Parenting is probably the hardest job an adult will undertake, but also the one for which the least amount of training and preparation is provided. By learning the most effective approaches, parents can reduce problem behaviours before they get out of control. (Webster-Stratton, 1992)

Problem behaviour among small children, in its many forms, adds stress to an already fraught family situation. Some problems such as soiling and bedwetting can place children at serious risk of abuse.

Although many of the interventions outlined in this chapter are based on the author's – ie, Buchanan's – experience and may as a result only be given the two-star rating, they are also supported by a solid evidence-base (eg, Webster-Stratton, 1992).

Slight modifications in a child's behaviour may keep a difficult family situation together while a more complex package of support is put in place. In other cases, a slight modification in a child's behaviour can set off a surprising avalanche of change: the children get to bed at night, parents feel better as they get more sleep, family arguments decrease and a child's behaviour improves at school.

Some of the most effective approaches for managing problem behaviour in young children are based on behavioural or learning theory. Learning theory suggests that problem behaviour is a result either of learning a response which causes difficulties, or of not having learnt the skill necessary to respond appropriately in the first place.

I WILL HAVE WHAT I WANT!

Jenny, who is 3, has a screaming fit in the shopping centre because she wants sweets. At first her mother says 'no', but because everybody is looking at her, she eventually gives Jenny sweets to keep her quiet. Two days later Jenny is again in the supermarket. Jenny is not stupid! She knows (she has learnt from her previous experience) that if she screams she will get what she wants, so she screams. Mother gives in and buys some sweets. Jenny has now learnt what seems to her to be a highly effective strategy for getting sweets. Mother may be able to tolerate the screaming, but when Jenny starts nursery school she also uses screaming to obtain what she wants. Not surprisingly, the staff object to this behaviour.

The challenge for Jenny's mother and the nursery school is to change Jenny's behaviour. The simplest strategy is to stop rewarding the screaming and start rewarding more socially acceptable behaviour.

The nursery decides to try a 'catch Jenny being good' routine. This involves taking special notice of Jenny when she is not screaming. Mother decides to teach Jenny a new skill – a new way to get what she wants. Mother plans ahead and takes along her own mother to help with the shopping. The plan is that if Jenny starts to scream, Granny will take Jenny straight home without any sweets. The routine is explained carefully to Jenny: 'If you scream you will go straight home with Granny; if you help me pack up at the food at the counter, I will buy some sweets for you when we are finished.' Jenny is not stupid. She quickly learns a new way of getting what she wants!

The principles of behavioural/cognitive behavioural interventions

Straight behavioural programmes (that is, those that do not involve cognitive ideas) are based on two ideas: helping children to *unlearn a behaviour* that is causing problems or to *learn a new behaviour* or skill to deal with a situation. Children learn in many ways, but one of the most effective is by being rewarded (being noticed, praised, getting tick marks in their lesson books, being given tangible rewards – sweets, stickers etc). Children also learn by copying the behaviour of others, particularly that of people who are important to them. Behavioural methods are useful where you can 'see' the problem behaviour and where the child is in an environment where the situation is controlled: at home with mother, or in a classroom setting.

Cognitive behavioural methods evolved from behavioural methods when it was realised that what a child was thinking or feeling (you cannot see a child's thoughts) directly influenced their behaviour.

- Tom, age 7, who stole a toy from a shop, had an internal dialogue with himself: 'I want that toy car ... no-one will notice me ... I will not get caught ... anyway I deserve a car 'cause all the other kids got one for Christmas.'
- Lisa, age 8, who was frightened about going to school, had another but different chat to herself: 'They are all big and clever at school, the teacher does not like me, I am very bad at my work, no-one likes me, they will beat me up.'

It is important to get at these 'cognitions' because the thoughts are directly influencing the behaviour. The hypothesis is that if you can change Tom's or Jenny's thoughts you will change their behaviour.

The many outcome studies on cognitive behavioural methods that have been used for a range of conditions and with all ages have amply rewarded this original idea. Cognitive methods are especially useful for slightly older children where a child has some choice and possible self-direction and where they have the capacity for independent thought, which can be translated into action. Central to the approach is sharing information about disorders and helping the child to develop the coping skills and strategies to manage him/herself. It is useful in depression, anxiety, anger management, and Attention Deficit Hyperactivity Disorder (ADHD). Linked to cognitive methods are approaches to help children to problem-solve.

Webster-Stratton (1992) and Herbert (1996a) both suggest to parents that:

> Rather than thinking of your child as having a problem or being a problem, it may help to think of her/him as trying to solve a problem. That behaviour you don't like may be her/his way of trying to deal not very successfully (for after all she/he's a learner), with one of life's difficulties. Let's try and see what she/he is trying to achieve. What are the developmental tasks she/he has to solve at this stage of life? (Herbert, 1996a)

Importance of engaging the family

The first task is to engage the parent/s and child. No matter how good the methods, the intervention will fail if the parent/s and child do not trust and believe in the person trying to help them. The timing has to be right. If parents are more concerned about where they are to get money for food that night or whether they are going to be evicted tomorrow, there is no point in trying to help them manage their children. Urgent concerns have to be dealt with first.

Partnership is central to the present way of working with families on behavioural programmes. Webster-Stratton and Herbert talk about this 'collaborative model':

> Collaboration implies a non-blaming, supportive, reciprocal relationship based on utilising equally the therapist's knowledge and the parents' unique strengths and perspectives … collaboration implies that parents actively participate in the setting of goals and therapy agenda and take responsibility with the therapist for solving their own or their family's problems … the therapist does not set him/herself up as the expert … the partnership between the parents and the therapist has the effect of giving back dignity, respect and self-control to parents who are often seeking help for their children's problems at a vulnerable time of low self-confidence and intense feelings of guilt and self-blame. (Herbert 1996a)

SOME BASIC PRINCIPLES OF BEHAVIOURAL INTERVENTIONS

Getting started

- Find out about the problem. You need to know where the behaviour happens, how often, for how long and under what conditions.
- Identify the desired outcomes, the goals of any intervention, for example, getting to bed at night … no tantrums.
- Find out what the child likes to do and what he/she is good at. You may be able to use this to motivate him/her.
- Specify the particular behaviour that is going to change, for example, getting out of bed and coming down to the TV, when you have gone to bed for the night.

Choosing the intervention strategies

- Reward is more effective than punishment.
- As long as the child is receiving some positive feedback, a behavioural programme cannot do any harm. Children should be set up to succeed.

- More negative behavioural techniques such as 'time-out' (where a child is set apart until he/she calms down) need to be used with extreme caution, if at all, particularly where parents may already be punitive or abusive.
- Parents need a strategy for when programmes do not work. For example: 'Have you ever tried being boring? … when Tim comes out of his bed in the middle of the night … just try being boring … let him sit with you but just do not notice him … when he looks sleepy put him back to bed.'

Monitoring

- Monitor carefully – at least once a week with young children.
- Reframe failures: 'It was hoped that Tim would stay in his bed all night, every night in the last week, but he only managed one night. Wow, what a success!'
- If a programme is not working or is becoming another stick to beat the child – drop it. Parents/child have not failed. The programme was wrong.

Did it work?

- How frequent is the problem behaviour now? What else can be done? Haven't Tim/parents done well!

What works in overcoming parental resistance?

Parents need to be strong to make the effort to tackle a child's problem behaviour. By the time the parent/s asks for help a child's behaviour may be so entrenched and the parent so depressed by the problems and other family adversities that they do not have the energy to be consistent or are too angry to be positive with their child. Dispirited parents implicitly feel their parenting is being criticised and are threatened by the professionals who come along and seem to 'know it all'. The following strategies have proved helpful in overcoming this resistance.

STRATEGIES FOR WORKING WITH DISPIRITED PARENTS

- *Dealing with feelings of parental failure.* Parents need to be reminded that children come in different shapes and sizes and with different personalities. Some children are easy to manage, others require more skill. It is a question of learning how best to manage a particular child, and this does not always come naturally.
- *Validating what they have achieved to date.* Many parents are coping with high levels of family adversity. Acknowledgement needs to be given for their resilience and overall coping skills.
- *Giving practical help first.* Help with day care, deal with the pressing concerns.
- *Giving hope that things can be different.* Demonstrate faith that the parent can change things.
- *Discussing the daily routine.* Find out what, in an ideal world, the mother/father would like to change.
- *Explaining that getting cross with a child can be like giving a child a bag of sweets and saying 'do that again'.* Children need attention like they need food, sleep and warmth, and if they cannot get attention for being good they will find a way of getting it by being bad.
- *Where a parent is being undermined by a critical partner or grandparent.* Meet with them and professionally validate the efforts they are making.
- *Helping a mother acknowledge she is nearing the end of her tether.* Ask the mother to hold out her hand straight in front of her. Although there can be medical reasons for this, the hands of highly stressed mothers will shake visibly. This can be used to demonstrate to partners and parents that more help is needed (it also applies to fathers).
- *Acknowledge that children can make you feel very angry.* Give parents a strategy to deal with themselves when they feel out of control, such as: 'You have every reason to feel angry but you don't want to hurt your kid ... so you get yourself out of the situation ... give yourself a break, get your Mum over ... if necessary lock yourself in the toilet, you are safer there than lashing out at the kid.'
- *Helping parents to plan.* Some child problems can be tough to overcome. Parents will have to plan a time when they are feeling strong enough to be consistent and to see things through. This is especially important with bedtime problems.

- *Using children to change parents' behaviour.* Picture contracts with 'smiley' face stickers for undertaking particular tasks can be very effective not only in changing the child's behaviour but for helping parents to learn new ways of managing a child's problems. These need to be monitored weekly by the professional. The parent and child have the credit for any success.

Particular interventions

Bedtime programmes

With younger children up to 3, health visitors are very skilled in helping children establish bedtime routines. The Royal College of Psychiatrists (Child and Adolescent Psychiatry Section) publish useful fact sheets for parents, teachers and young people, including one on sleep problems in childhood and adolescence (www.rcpsych. ac.uk/info/mhqu/newmhqu7.htm) (Tel: 020 7235 2351 Fax: 020 7245 1231). These involve signalling that it is bedtime by a regular bedtime routine: bath, drink, night-time clothes, bed; ensuring the child is warm and comfortable; saying goodnight. If the child awakes, minimal attention is given. Older toddlers can be persistent when disagreeing with a parent that it is bedtime. The toddler who repeatedly gets out of his/her bed and joins the parent/s makes the parents cross and irritable and leaves the child distressed and tired. These parents may need some help. There are two possible approaches.

PLANNING A DIFFICULT WEEK/WEEKEND

The first task is to find out how often the child has problems going to bed, whether the child is distressed or ill, and whether the conditions in which the child is expected to sleep are possible for sleep – eg, whether the room is warm and quiet enough, or that a parent does not return from work late and want to play. Parents are then encouraged to plan ahead so that they have at least a month when their lives are reasonably settled – they should not try to sort things out over Christmas. They will need to be able to devote at least a weekend, without getting much sleep themselves, to getting the child to bed and keeping him/her there. The bedtime routine is agreed with the worker, including a regular time for bed every night. The various health/safety checks are agreed, eg, the length of time parents are prepared to leave the child crying without checking.

The parents are encouraged to put the child to bed following their regular routine. If the child gets up, very quietly and gently they take the child back to his/her bed with the minimum fuss. Every time the child gets out of bed the process is repeated. This pattern is repeated night after night until staying in bed is established.

Some parents find the above routine too stressful. If there are any hints of maltreatment the approach is not recommended. Another well-tested approach is setting up a bedtime contract with the child (Webster and Buchanan, 1982). In this programme the child effectively trains the parent how to respond. The bonus of bedtime programmes is that in around 75 per cent of cases they work very well. A routine will be established within a month, which is then supported by the child's own biological clock. The child feels tired at the set bedtime. Less tired children perform better at school; parents with more time together in the evenings may become less stressed; without a child in their bed at night, they too may sleep better. In the remaining 25 per cent there may be more complex problems.

CHILD'S BEDTIME CONTRACT

As before, details are taken of the bedtime problem, the physical condition of the child and any health or other worries. The child's bedroom is checked as well as the family routine.

With the child and parent's help, the worker draws up a picture contract with the child that reflects the existing routine. The reward is a 'smiley' face – a pink dot on a card with a face drawn on it. The child asks for this in the morning and the parent sticks it on.

If the child gets out of bed parents are encouraged to act 'boring' and allow the child to sit with them with minimal attention until the child can gently be put back to bed. After a few days – the child may need to be encouraged by half a 'smiley' face' for nearly succeeding – most children manage to remain in their beds as long as the family routine remains constant. After a month, the child's biological clock kicks in and the programme gradually gets forgotten, and is only re-introduced if the waking behaviour returns.

One glass of milk

A bedtime story
Three bears

Mum reads a story

I go to bed …and stay there until the sun come up

Week	Mon	Tues	Wed	Thur	Fri	Sat	Sun
One	☺						
Two	☺	☺	☺	☺	☺		
Three	☺	☺	☺	☺	☺	☺	
Four	☺	☺	☺	☺	☺	☺	☺

Well done me! I am very clever!

Figure 16 **My bedtime plan**

Focused activity for very active young children
This approach, unlike the bedtime contract, has not been formally evaluated, but in Buchanan's experience, using this or similar approaches with primary school-age children, brought improvement in two out of three cases.

JIMMY'S GETTING READY FOR SCHOOL PROJECT

Jimmy, age 6, was the eldest of three boys (the others were 4 and 2) in a fairly chaotic family. Jimmy never sat still. Getting Jimmy organised for school in the morning as well as getting his brother ready to go to nursery and the youngest child in the pushchair to take them there, was a Herculean task for his mother. Jimmy would lose his shoes, fight with his brother, upset the baby. Mother, as a result, would lose her cool and Jimmy would arrive in school in a state of high arousal. Predictably he could not concentrate on his work, and easily got into disputes with other boys. Suspension was a strong possibility.

- *Assessment and intervention.* A review was taken of an 'average' morning. With mother's help a timetable of things to do before school was decided. The tasks included preparing his school bag the night before and, in the morning, getting up, dressed, washed, coming downstairs for cereal and milk and putting himself and his coat/schoolbag together. This was set out as a big picture contract in Jimmy's room, with stars as a reward and a football sticker for achieving five stars. After school, if he had completed the morning task, his mother put a star on his chart – perhaps half a star for tasks half completed. The social worker called once a week to check that the programme was working.
- *Outcome.* The main benefit of the programme was that Jimmy's behaviour improved at school and he settled down to his school work. The secondary outcome was that home life in the mornings was less frenetic for all the children. Mother on her own initiative used a similar programme for the younger boy. In the long term Jimmy continued to have problems in school but he was not suspended.

Cognitive behavioural approaches for modifying aggressive behaviour

My brother said I hit him, but I didn't. My father growled at me. I got mad with Dad. When I get angry it's like I've got a VOLCANO in my tummy. (A story by L, age 9; Whitehouse and Pudney, 1996)

Children often have problems with anger. Central to cognitive behavioural approaches is that is it OK to feel angry but it's not OK to hurt others, yourself or things around you. Many of the strategies are about helping children recognise when they are angry (the physiological signs), when they are getting of control and when they need to use strategies to calm themselves down. Whitehouse and Pudney's book, *A volcano in my tummy*, is full of useful ideas. The following two strategies also worked well in practice.

FIGURE 17 TWO BEHAVIOURAL STRATEGIES

1 Wait for the green light

Wayne was in trouble at school for fighting. There were many other family problems.

Wayne's school problems were the last straw for his family. Wayne was seen by the social worker for three sessions.

Session 1: Feeling angry ... recognising the physical signs. Role-playing feeling angry ... clenched fists, grinding jaws, shoulders hunched up around your ears ... and then relaxing. Homework: practise at school.

Session 2: The traffic light. Red for danger (I am very angry) Amber (for stop and think) Green (I am now calmer). Role-play touching the card (drawing of the traffic light) as a reminder. Homework: practise at school.

Session 3: Follow-up in two weeks.

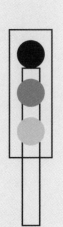

2 Time out

Terry, age 8, lived with his parents and older sister. When angry he completely lost control and smashed anything he could get his hands on. The idea of 'time-out', or taking himself off to his room to calm down, appealed to Terry. He was taught to recognise when he was feeling angry. Thereafter, whenever he felt himself losing control he would announce to his family 'I am very angry, I am taking time-out. Please do not disturb me.' The strategy worked well. Terry remained in control. His family respected his need for time-out.

Strategies to stop stealing in primary-aged children

There are a range of reasons why young children steal. Farrington (1979) has shown that very large numbers of children admit to having committed an indictable offence. One reason why children steal is that they think they will not get caught. Statistics show that this is a fair assessment. We also know that looking back, many of the persistent offenders started offending before the age of criminal responsibility. On the other hand most children who are caught and cautioned never offend again, so there are very good reasons for increasing the likelihood of them getting caught. The aim of the following strategies is to limit the opportunities for stealing, increase the likelihood of getting caught and to raise the child's awareness of what could happen if they do get caught.

STOPPING JIMMY STEALING

Jimmy is stealing money from home. The local policeman has been around to see his parents. They are already in touch with the social worker about other matters but ask for help 'to sort Jimmy out'. Parents are instructed to count their money every night and to make a show of doing this in front of the family. As Jimmy is also stealing from local shops, parents are instructed to go to the local shop and return the goods with Jimmy in hand. In addition, a detailed plan is made to divert Jimmy away from tempting areas, for example, shopping centres. Plans are also made to limit unsupervised play times.

The happy and the sad face at the window

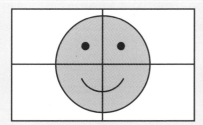 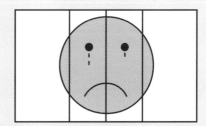

Every time that Jimmy is tempted to steal he has a choice: the happy face or the sad face. The choice is there every time he takes something that does not belong to him. He alone is responsible for what happens to him. The card is given to Jimmy to keep in his pocket to remind him of the choices he is making.

It feels bad because it does not belong to me
The second strategy involves leaving a 50p piece on the table and suggesting to Jimmy that he might like to pick it up and put it his pocket when the social worker goes out of the room.

The social worker then returns and tells Jimmy: 'That 50p feels bad … it feels wrong … it does not belong to you … it will cause problems if it is not returned … you could get into serious trouble.' The social worker then goes out of the room and tells Jimmy he might like to take the coin out of his pocket and replace it on the table. Coming back … 'That feels better … the worry has gone … the weight is lifted … You might be tempted to take something … you might even take it, but if you are lucky you have a second chance … you can put it back.'

School phobics and school truants

Children miss school for a variety of reasons. Some children are genuinely frightened of going to school (the phobic child) and some children do not go to school because what they can do outside school is more interesting than going to school (the truant). Rutter (1975) shows the clear divide between the child who is phobic and the child who truants. The phobic child generally stays at home. He/she may have a parent who is themselves agoraphobic, or a parent who is ill. The child may feel he/she has to stay at home to look after the sick parent. Generally the truant goes out with his/her friends.

STRATEGY ONE: THE PARENT OF THE PHOBIC CHILD – PLANNING TO BE STRONG

After a careful assessment of all the issues – is there any reason why Jenny did not want to go to school? Is bullying a problem, trouble with teachers, difficulties with school work? Is Jenny generally fit and healthy? Is a firm approach likely to work? The first approach is to work with the parent/s, who have to plan to be strong enough to persuade Jenny that she has to go to school. Parent/s role-play being firm: 'I am sorry Jenny but today you are going to school … your Mother/Father is here to make sure and Mrs Smith your teacher is waiting for you at school.' Parent is told: 'You are churning inside … you are worried … but you are not going to let it show … Jenny will say she is ill … You waver … but only for a moment … you know she is not ill … you are not going to get into an argument … today is the day Jenny is going to school.' Plans are laid with the parent when partner or a helper is around to assist and the teacher is primed to be ready at the school.

STRATEGY TWO: THE PHOBIC CHILD – PLANNING TO BE STRONG

'… so I'll get up, clean my teeth, have breakfast, be sick and then set off'

With older phobic children, they need to get back into control of their emotions. Some are quite frightened by their physical response to the fear. These children may have highly phobic mothers or fathers who are not able to be strong. Again, after a careful assessment to ensure there are no adverse school conditions, the child is encouraged to develop a routine that includes her anxiety. The following is based on a real case. Liz was a very intelligent 11-year-old. Liz liked school and enjoyed the lessons but she and her mother worked themselves up into a frenzy every morning resulting in both of them being physically sick and Liz not going to school.

'This sickness is tough … this sickness is getting in the way of what you want to do … it is taking hold of your life … do you want it to control your life for ever?… why not have a go at being the master? Why not build being sick into your morning routine? You can't stop being sick, but being sick won't stop you going to school. You get up, clean your teeth, eat something, and be sick before you go to school. Once you have been sick you will feel better, so you take yourself to school.'

After a week Liz stopped being sick. The second week, however, she developed diarrhoea. 'OK that's tough … but you don't want it to be master of you any more than the sickness … so you get up, clean your teeth, eat something, go to the toilet and put on a sanitary towel in case of accidents … now you know you are safe so you can go to school.' By the third week Liz was attending school regularly without sickness or diarrhoea. The social worker went back weekly for a few weeks to support her.

Young truants can also be very demanding. The challenge with the truant is to make going to school more fun than staying away and to ensure that if Johnny 'skives' he will get caught. The schools play an important part in this partnership with parents. There is considerable evidence that where schools have attendance policies, this considerably reduces levels of truancy (Collins, 1998).

Feeding problems

Dorota Iwaniec's book, *The emotionally abused and neglected child*, and her studies on 'failure to thrive' are the key texts here (Iwaniec, 1995). Minor eating problems can easily develop into major food refusal when children have a period of 'being off their food' (Webster-Stratton 1992).

'YOU CAN'T GET DOWN, KATE, UNTIL YOU FINISH YOUR DINNER'

Many parents feel that it is important that children 'finish' a plate of food. Forcing children to eat food they do not want can be extremely dangerous and lead to major food battles and food refusal. Once this stage is reached the first step is to ascertain how severe the problem is.

If weight or weight loss is not a major problem it should be considered that many children have periods of faddiness: they may have been ill or they may be worried about something at school or at home. They become a little depressed and go off their food. An authoritarian approach forcing Kate (age 4) to eat or to finish a meal is totally counter productive. Kate is more likely to recover her eating zeal if the pressure is removed and she is allowed to eat what she likes – children can live on ice-cream and chips for several weeks. Kate will do better still if she is ignored while she eats and/or she shares her meals with other children. Gradually as the battle is forgotten she will return to normal eating patterns.

If weight loss is a problem, the GP should always be involved, particularly with small children. These children may need specialist paediatric or psychiatric care.

Wetting (Morgan, 1981) and soiling (Buchanan, 1992)

Bedwetting, particularly among boys, is very common. Around one in five wet the bed at age 5 and around one in ten still wet the bed between the ages of 6–9. In some families there may be a family history of bedwetting. Soiling is less common but around 3 children in every 100 will be soiling on entering primary school. The consequences of both wetting and soiling problems for children are severe. Very often the children smell and become the butt of bullying in school.

At home a dangerous vicious circle develops. In an abusive family, the child's problem will increase the level of stress in the family, which in turn will increase the level of soiling and bedwetting in the child. Urinary infections are also very common and the doctor should always check this possibility.

Management of the problem

It is important that children should not be made to feel bad about what has happened, should not be teased by others in the family, and should not be punished or made to think they have been naughty. But studies show that when children manage the bedwetting by cleaning up their bed (a draw-sheet across the middle of the bed under and over the child and lined in polythene can make this easier), this puts them in control and eases tensions in the family. Similarly the more a child can do to clean him/herself up, the more tension goes from a soiling problem. This can be done by teaching children to wash out their mistakes and to put their pants straight into the washing machine. Another strategy is to take a 'security' bag with clean underclothes and wet-wipes to school in case of accidents.

Treatment

For children from the age of 8 and above, the most effective treatment is the bell-alarm. These are often available through school nurses. They are placed in a child's bed and the child is awoken when he/she wets the bed. Gradually the child learns to awaken before the alarm goes off.

For soilers, treatment is more complex. Most soilers suffer from constipation and this needs to be regularly checked and treated by the GP or paediatrician. Effectively they get a blockage in the bowel. The soiling, which may be leakage around the blockage, can be mistaken for diarrhoea when quite the reverse is the problem.

After checking that the child has no physical problems, many children, particularly younger children, can be treated by a reward programme for successful defecation. Since 'holding on' leads to constipation, they must not be rewarded for being clean. Children over the age of 8 who soil can have intermittent problems until adolescence when problems clear up, except in exceptional cases.

Key messages

- Children manifest their distress in many ways. It is a communication that we need to hear. Although we may not always know what the child is trying to say, we need to keep listening.
- Behaviour problems can be a manifestation of distress but what caused the problem may be very different from what is maintaining the problem.
- Ongoing behaviour problems present both the parent/s and child with considerable difficulties and all we can do is to try and help them live more happily together.
- Specialists have a wider range of help available. The approaches suggested here are those that can be undertaken by front-line workers and those with the best evidence that they will be effective. They will not be successful in all cases. Some problems like wetting and soiling can be very resistant to treatment.
- Behavioural methods may produce a miraculous change in the overall well-being of a family and child after which everything appears to slot into place. It is more likely, however, that the gains achieved (wetting the bed four nights out of seven instead of seven out of seven) will act as a sticking plaster that helps the child and family come through the worst of a 'bad' patch. With many families known to family support workers, this is a respectable aim.

10 Managing common adolescent emotional and behavioural problems

The two most difficult times of life are when you are a teenager and when you have to care for a teenager. (Narramore and Lewis, 1990)

Many adolescents pass through the transition from childhood to adulthood with the minimum of difficulties. A few find the process more difficult. The physical, intellectual and psychological maturation that comes at this time places great strain on the young person's resources and those of their carer. Earlier problems may resurface.

Throughout this demanding period, young people have to learn the necessary skills to cope as successful adults. This social adolescence requires a certain amount of experimentation – the need to learn for yourself. While adolescents may be rebellious with adults, they seem to be over-compliant with peers.

At this time, young people require adults who listen, are available for them, show respect, offer advice and guidance but are not over-controlling or over-authoritarian. Parents, almost without knowing, balance out the risks for their young by introducing new protective experiences – the son may be introduced to a new activity with a new group of peers to divert him from a potentially delinquent group of friends.

For all young people as they experiment with the dangers of their age, 'harm-reduction' is a key strategy. Young people need accurate information about the risks they are taking – drugs, sex, relationships – so that they are equipped to make more competent decisions.

For young people with more serious problems the following programmes, many based on cognitive behavioural principles, may prove helpful. There are of course other approaches, but these generally require more specialist knowledge and/or medication.

Feeling down and depressed

Mood swings are common in adolescence. If a young person becomes very depressed – to the extent that it affects their sleeping, eating and normal way of life – and/or if the young person admits to suicidal ideas, that person needs specialist help (Graham and Hughes, 1997).

In between clinical depression and the normal adolescent mood swings is the adolescent who is 'moderately depressed'. Cognitive behavioural approaches are very effective with moderately depressed young people aged 11–18 (Harrington et al, 1998). Findings from studies in Manchester and Birmingham show that depressed young people have three main sets of symptoms:

- *negative styles of thinking*, which include low self-esteem, negative attributions (when things go wrong it is all my fault) and negative cognitions (it is all hopeless, there is no point trying)
- *difficulties with social relationships*
- *behavioural symptoms of depression* such as poor sleep and inactivity.

The following programme has proved helpful with some of these young people (Wood et al, 1996). After a formal assessment, ten sessions of treatment are led by a child mental health professional who has had attended a two-day brief introductory course and some supervised training of cognitive behavioural methods. Each session involves an introduction, tasks, practice and homework assignments. The programme teaches young people how to identify and monitor their emotions, and self-reinforce or reward themselves when they have achieved tasks. This may involve activity scheduling – that is, increasing the number of pleasant activities they engage in; social problem solving; and strategies for reducing depressive thinking for handling future problems. Harrington (in Wood et al, 1996) concludes that:

> Cognitive behavioural therapy is an effective treatment for many depressed young people but it is not a cure-all and needs to be conceptualised as just one part of the treatment strategy.

Recognising suicidal behaviour

The volatility of young people's emotions can be very frightening. A young person may be 'moderately depressed' one day and dangerously depressed the next. Suicidal behaviour is very common when an adolescent is experiencing a major depression. Men are at greater risk of committing suicide while women are more likely to commit acts of deliberate self-harm, though this gap has closed (Hawton, 1986). Studies of young people in public care have shown that suicidal behaviour is not unusual and may often go unrecognised (Buchanan et al, 1993).

The Health Advisory Service summarises the main risk factors as follows.

RISK FACTORS FOR SUICIDE AND SUICIDAL BEHAVIOUR

- depression
- economic and social pressures
- alcohol and substance abuse
- custody
- bullying
- (perhaps) rural isolation
- physical and sexual abuse
- previous acts of deliberate self-harm
- family problems/cultural conflicts (Asian women are over-represented in self-poisoning)

Once a child has undertaken an act of deliberate self-harm, there are various risk lists to access the likelihood of a repeated attempt. Among these is the PATHOS screening questionnaire for use after an act of deliberate self-harm (see Kingsbury, in Health Advisory Service, 1994).

PATHOS SCREENING QUESTIONNAIRE

(P) Have you had **P**roblems for longer than one month?

(A) Were you **A**lone in the house when you overdosed?

(T) Did you plan the overdose for more than **T**hree hours?

(HO) Are you feeling **Ho**peless about the future: that things won't get much better?

(S) Were you feeling **S**ad for most of the time before the overdose?

Although risk lists are helpful, each individual needs to be assessed on their own situation. The following are the recommendations of the Royal College of Psychiatrists (1982) in respect of child and adolescent deliberate self-harm (DSH):

- direct child psychiatry involvement in all cases of child deliberate self-harm
- rapidity of response dependent on resources
- GPs to be kept fully informed
- hospital admission desirable in cases of DSH
- under 14s admitted to paediatric ward; 14–16s to adolescent ward
- hospital staff responsible for gaining parental consent to psychiatric assessment; non-medical staff may carry out assessment; consultant psychiatrist retains responsibility for service
- social services involvement may be necessary in some cases
- psychiatric inpatient treatment may be necessary in some cases.

Further recommendations were made in 1996, indicating that DSH in the under 16s should always be taken seriously. Child protection procedures should reflect the fact that DSH is often the route through which child abuse and neglect come to light. Assessment and treatment formulation plans should address the child's continuing self-harm impulses, overall mental health, psychosocial situation and parental ability. Consultant child and adolescent psychiatrists have a responsibility to inform purchasing authorities of the resource and training needs of their service. They should develop and oversee the implementation of DSH guidelines (Sutton, 1996).

Managing anxiety and fears

> Fears and anxieties in children are a normal part of growing up ... the question is does anxiety consistently inhibit functioning to an extent that the child is overly distressed and/or experiences significant impairments in daily functioning? (Ronan and Deane, 1998)

Children with extreme fears or prolonged bouts of anxieties should be referred for specialist care. Many children have short periods of anxiety, perhaps relating to school stresses such as examinations. Simple cognitive behavioural techniques can be helpful for these children. These techniques teach the child strategies for managing anxiety, reducing personal distress and increasing mastery and coping skills.

The following is a brief outline of the techniques. Using the ABC framework (A = factors that arouse the anxiety in the child; B = the child's fear response both physical and emotional expression; C = the consequence) the child is helped to use the four-step FEAR plan:

LIZZIE AND HER FEAR PLAN

Lizzie is coming up to her GCSEs. She gets very anxious about examinations. This makes her upset because she knows she is sabotaging herself and her chances. She uses the FEAR plan:

(F) Feeling frightened? (awareness of bodily cues and identifying what is causing the anxiety). I can feel myself tense up when I think about examinations ... I get all panicky and then cannot concentrate on my revision.

(E) Expecting bad things to happen? (identifying the internal self-talk and then correcting the false ideas). I will fail this exam ... I will fail all my examinations ... I am a total failure. Correction: why do I think that I will fail this examination ... I passed the last one ... I am actually doing quite well at school ... even if I fail this examination I can take it again. My revision is going quite well this time.

(A) Attitudes and actions that can help (coping and problem-solving strategies). Well I have been working quite hard ... I need to keep to my revision schedule ... I am not good at remembering the dates so I will put them on a card and revise these at the last minute ... deep breathing seems to help when I get into an examination ...

(R) Result and rewards (self-evaluation and reward/coping in failure). I have managed two sessions of revision without getting panic attacks ... this is not too bad ... but I could still do better ... I must work on relaxing and deep breathing because I am sabotaging myself ... I could do better ... but I can do it now I know how.

Including the parents can improve outcomes from the FEAR therapy. Parents are taught how to reward courageous acts and how to ignore as far as possible the child's excessive anxiety; how to prompt the child to follow the FEAR plan; how to disguise and manage their own anxiety; and family-based problem-solving strategies.

Managing anger

There a number of anger management programmes specifically designed for adolescents. Many of these programmes are based on the work of Novaco (1975). The aim of these programmes is to lower the likelihood of aggressive behaviour by helping the person become aware of the signs of impending potential hostile arousal and then teaching strategies of self-control.

In programmes by D'Zurilla and Goldfried (1971) adolescents are helped to identify their aggressive behaviour and then recognise the conditions which provoke and maintain it. There are various stages in anger management.

ANGER MANAGEMENT

- Recognising problem situations when they occur ... this is making me angry.
- Resisting the temptation to act impulsively ... Cool it ... It is cleverer to think this one out.
- What are the issues that are making me angry? ... What problems have I to cope with?
- What are the possible things I could do in this situation? ... What solution is likely to lead to the most positive consequence?
- Well I thought it out and did it ... How did it go? ... That was OK, it went well.

Loss and bereavement

Fewer children today experience death in the immediate family than in the past but they experience loss and bereavement in other ways: when parents part; when they are separated from those they love; when they go into public care; when they have a chronic illness. Observations have confirmed that there are three stages of grief (Goodman and Scott, 1997).

- *Initial crisis response.* With shock, denial and disbelief. There may be emotional numbness and feelings of detachment; thoughts and behaviour may be focused on the person who is gone.
- *Emotional disorganisation.* Sadness, crying, anger and resentment, feelings of despair, disappointment, hopelessness and worthlessness. There may also be poor sleep and appetite and sometimes feelings of guilt and self-blame.

- *Adjustment* to the loss becomes evident when anxiety is reduced, there is increased enjoyment of life and greater involvement in everyday activities.

Responses vary and children have different strategies for coping which need to be respected. Some children may not be ready to talk about their sadness, others may move between the different stages or temporarily go back a stage. Listening, being available, giving permission both to talk about and *not* to talk about their sadness and the person they have lost, are usually the most effective strategies to help the child.

CHILDREN'S UNDERSTANDING OF DEATH

The following information is based on Kane's studies (1979) of how children 'generally' respond to death.

- *Under 4 years*: Most children from the age of 3 are familiar with the word death but their understanding is limited. They do not understand the permanence of death. They may think a parent has gone to hospital because they were angry with them. They may pester the surviving parent: 'When is mummy/daddy coming back?' They may show their distress by separation anxiety, wetting, loss of appetite, disturbed sleep, clinging behaviour and a lowered resistance to infections.
- *5–10 years*: Most 5-year-olds know that death means separation and that they will feel lonely. They may also realise that dead people cannot move, but at this age the finality of death eludes them. It is not until age 7 or 8 that children develop concepts of 'life', and a more or less clear concept of 'death'. They recognise that every living organism eventually dies.
- *8–9 years*: Children realise that dying can apply to them. Children at this age can be helped if they realise that on death, pain will go. Disturbances of emotion and behaviour are common. In the year after the loss of a parent as many as 50 per cent of children manifest problems such as school refusal, stealing and poor concentration, and 30 per cent still have problems two years on.
- *Adolescents*: By 12 years most children understand that a dead body is different from a living body; they understand the permanence of death; and they may have their own theories to explain death. They express their grief more like adults. Same sex children may have difficulty separating from the deceased parent. There is a loss of identity and there are the big 'Why?' questions. Some adolescents can display an apparent lack of feeling or indifference.

Acute or prolonged reactions to bereavement may benefit from medical help.

Most studies show that losing a parent through death is essentially different from losing a parent through divorce or separation although the initial pain may be similar. Most children who lose a parent through death suffer no serious psychological consequences in the long term (Rodgers and Pryor, 1998).

Post-traumatic stress disorder (PTSD)

Following major emotional or physical upheavals such as disasters, accidents or bereavement, a high proportion of children experience several distressing reactions including anxiety, fear and depression. It is now acknowledged that many actually manifest symptoms of Post Traumatic Stress Disorder. (Herbert, 1996b)

In recent years, it has been found that large numbers of children who have been sexually abused suffer from post-traumatic stress disorder (PTSD), as well as many of those who have been physically abused. Around 60 per cent of those involved in disasters also suffer from PTSD. Children witness around 10–20 per cent of murders (most of these arise out of domestic disputes). PTSD may therefore be much more common than previously thought. It is hard to detect PTSD in a child who can appear well behaved as they sit quietly preoccupied with their own thoughts. Most affected children do not tell their parents.

The degree of the trauma influences the extent of the symptoms. Those experiencing life-threatening events tend to be the worst affected. Similar traumas can have very different effects on different individuals. Resilient children who have a good relationship with one parent, a cohesive and harmonious family and a wider support network of peers and teachers, may be better able to cope. On the other hand, children with family problems, social disadvantage and difficulties with their peers are likely to be less resilient (Deblinger et al, 1990).

Key criteria

- The child has experienced a major trauma that would be upsetting for everyone.
- The child re-experiences the trauma by one of the following: recurrent vivid flashbacks of the event; recurrent dreams of the event; behaving or feeling as if the event is recurring triggered by a mental reminder of the event.

- The child becomes less responsive or less involved in day-to-day activities, or feels detached or estranged from others or seems unable to experience any feelings.
- There will be at least two of the following symptoms in the child that were not present before the traumatic experience: hyper-alertness, or an exaggerated startle response; sleep disturbance; guilt feelings about being a survivor; memory problems or difficulty in concentrating; avoidance of activities that remind the child of the trauma; intensification of symptoms when in a situation that reminds the child of the event.

THE SINKING OF THE *JUPITER*

In 1988 the cruise ship *Jupiter*, carrying 400 children and teachers, sank outside Athens. Despite the horrendous trauma, all but one child and one teacher survived. A study by Yule and colleagues (1990) compared three groups of girls: those who went on the cruise; those who had wanted to go but could not get a place; and another group of girls in another school. It was found that surviving children experienced repetitive, intrusive thoughts about the event that happened in quiet periods, such as at bedtime; fears of the dark, nightmares, waking throughout the night; separation difficulties (even amongst adolescents); not letting parents out of sight; anger and irritability; difficulty talking to peers and parents; concentration and memory problems; fearfulness about possible dangers; a sense of the fragility of life, pessimism; changed priorities, lack of planning ahead; changes in values; fears associated with specific aspects of the trauma; avoidance of threatening situations; survivor guilt; depression (especially in adolescents) and suicidal thoughts; panic attacks.

What those around can do to help

Following a trauma most children and young people want to be with their parents and friends. *Critical Incident Stress Debriefing* (Dyregrov, 1991) after traumas has been used to share feelings, experiences and reactions in the privacy of the group setting. In fact, whether debriefing meets its stated objectives of reducing traumatic symptoms can be difficult to evaluate and only a very few studies have been completed to date. Findings from these studies have been mixed, with some studies suggesting that at best debriefing has no benefit in reducing traumatic symptoms and in some circumstances could possibly be harmful, that is, in prolonging symptoms (Rose et al, 2001).

The best way of helping a child is for the 'significant person' in the child's life to be 'available' to give permission to talk (or not to talk) if he/she wants, to normalise feelings – 'it is OK to feel sad … it is OK not to feel sad … it is normal to feel jittery … it is normal to get flashbacks … it is normal not to get flashbacks' – and to clarify distortions and misconceptions. Schools should be informed and as far as possible those around need to be sensitive and accepting of short periods of difficult behaviour. Difficulties getting to sleep can be overcome by listening to tape music or story tapes. Bad dreams can be retold during the day giving a happy ending (Goodman and Scott, 1997). If problems persist, however, children should be referred for specialist help.

Where children have experienced major disruption following war, such as refugees, distressed behaviour may also be related to the disruption and concern about the future. Children's basic needs should be met first.

Substance abuse

The majority of young people will experiment with alcohol and/or drugs yet go on to lead 'normal' lives. In problematic drug and alcohol use there are two broad areas of concern:

- where drug or alcohol use is negatively affecting school and/or family life
- where use is a danger to health.

In general, problematic behaviour such as truancy and crime begins at an earlier age (13.8 and 14.5 years) than drug use (16.2 years generally, and 19.9 years for any 'hard' drugs). It should be of some concern, however, that such problematic use is associated with preceding emotional and behavioural problems, which in turn may be related to harsh and authoritarian (affectionless control) parenting (Clausen, 1996). Although the evidence suggests that the most powerful predictor of teenage drug use and delinquent behaviour is similar behaviour by peers, those friendships are in turn predicted by earlier negative parenting (Garnier and Stein, 2002). There is, however, also evidence to suggest that high male unemployment within the community and social deprivation also play a part.

Strategies to improve parenting, particularly among those showing early signs of conduct or attention deficit disorders, may help at a preventive level, combined with programmes that foster community involvement. Models of good projects that have been found to work in the US include **Across Ages** (LoScinto et al, 1996) – a school and community-based drug prevention programme for young people age 9–13 years. This is one of the model programmes recommended by Substance Abuse and Mental Health Services Administration (SAMHSA), US Department of Health and Human Services. Full details of all these programmes and how to implement them can be seen on the SAMHSA website (www.modelprograms.samhsa.gov).

Table 17 **Mentoring and community service to reduce risk factors for drug abuse**

Studies	Intervention	Outcomes	Why it works – possible mechanisms
***Across Ages Taylor and Bressler (2000) The overall goal of the programme is to increase the protective factors for high-risk students (age 9–13) in order to prevent, reduce or delay the use of alcohol, tobacco and other drugs and the problems associated with such use. Also seeks to strengthen the bonds between adults and youth and provide opportunities for positive community involvement.	Uses mentors, age 55 and above, community service activities, family workshops and activities to increase young people's knowledge of health and substance abuse and to foster healthy attitudes, intentions and behaviour toward drug use.	Evaluation with comparative groups showed that there was: improved knowledge about and reactions to drug use; decreased alcohol and tobacco use; increased school attendance; decreased suspensions from school and improved grades; improved attitudes toward adults. *But note the level of mentor involvement was positively related to improvement on various outcomes measures.*	The unique and highly effective feature of Across Ages is the pairing of older adult mentors with young adolescents, specifically youth making the transition to middle school. The involvement in community service also appears to be important.

Another SAMHSA programme uses a family therapy approach. Again, the focus of the approach is preventing children and young people becoming involved in substance abuse.

Table 18 **Brief Strategic Family Therapy (BSFT) to reduce risk factors for substance abuse**

Studies	Intervention	Outcomes	Why it works – possible mechanisms
Brief Strategic Family Therapy (BSFT) Szapocznik and Hervis (2001) For the elimination of substance abuse risk factors in children and adolescents age 6–17.	It targets conduct problems, associations with antisocial peers, early substance use, problematic *family* relations. 8–12 weekly sessions. The programme fosters parental leadership, appropriate parental involvement, mutual support among parenting figures, *family* communication, problem-solving, clear rules and consequences, nurturing and shared responsibility for *family* problems. In addition, the programme provides specialided outreach strategies to bring families into therapy.	Based on three randomised controlled trials with different populations (Hispanic and African-American). *Outcomes* • 42 per cent improvement in conduct problems • 75 per cent reduction in marijuana use • 58 per cent reduction in association with antisocial peers • 75 per cent retained in programme.	This is another programme that starts early and has a multi-focus also involving the family.

The following approach targets the more difficult young people – chronically violent, substance abusing young offenders age 12–17 years.

Table 19 **Multi-Systematic Therapy (MST) for chronically violent, substance abusing offenders**

Studies	Intervention	Outcomes	Why it works – possible mechanisms
***Multisystemic Therapy* (MST) (Henggeler et al, 1998) MST is a family-oriented, home-based programme that targets chronically violent, substance-abusing juvenile offenders 12–17 years old. It uses methods that promote positive social behaviour and decrease antisocial behaviour, including substance use, to change how youth function in their natural settings (ie, home, school and neighbourhood).	Therapists have small caseloads of four to six families; work as a team; are available 24 hours a day, 7 days a week; and provide services at times convenient to the family. The average treatment involves about 60 hours of contact during a 4-month period. Over the long term produces considerable cost savings over other social services.	Based on several randomised controlled trials with diverse populations of serious and chronic juvenile offenders, and follow-up of two to four years after completing: • decreased adolescent substance use • decreased adolescent psychiatric symptoms • 25–70 per cent reduced long-term re-arrest rates. • 47–64 per cent reduced out-of-home placement • increased school attendance.	The home-based model of service delivery reduces barriers that keep families from accessing services. Also the multi-system focus and intensive nature of programme.

In the UK, the Effective Interventions Unit of the Department of Health has identified the following interventions as effective in reducing drug use:

Most effective:

- behaviour therapy
- culturally sensitive counselling
- family therapy.

Less effective but still some success:

- general drug treatment programmes
- therapeutic community and residential care
- school-based programmes that use life skills development and are targeted at high-risk groups.

Purely educational programmes are generally ineffective in reducing drug use.

Programmes also need to address risky behaviours

Young people with problem drug- or alcohol-related behaviours are also more at risk of HIV, unwanted pregnancies, sexually transmitted diseases, accidents and so on, as well as offending behaviour. At both preventive and reductive levels, programmes need to ensure that these young people take steps to reduce the risks associated with mind-altering substances.

Seek professional help

Young people using Class A drugs (such as heroin, cocaine and crack) need professional help. Current government strategy to improve GP and primary care services and reduce waiting times at treatment centres may improve outcomes.

Risk of offending

In this short volume there is not space to look at other juvenile justice programmes in depth. It is important to remember that young people at risk of criminal activity should not be mixed with convicted adolescents. Several studies have found that placing antisocial adolescents in a deviant peer group can make their problems worse. Non-offending antisocial young people need to have separate programmes from re-offenders.

Figure 19 **Effectiveness of non-juvenile-justice treatments**

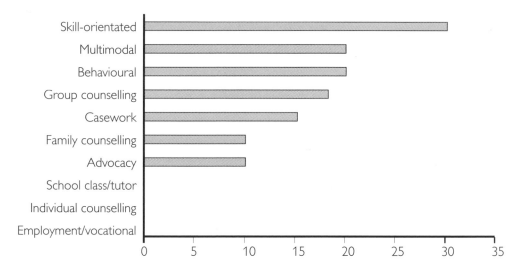

Figure 20 **Effectiveness of different types of youth justice interventions**

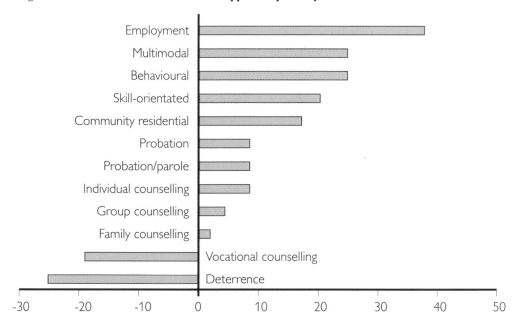

The following bar charts (adapted from Rutter et al, 1998; original diagrams from Lipsey, 1995) are based on an analysis of a large number of studies. They show the percentage of antisocial young people which improved under each type of treatment. The first bar chart looks at non-youth justice treatments and the second at juvenile justice treatments. In both cases the best results come from behavioural, skill-orientated and multimodal (packages of care) methods.

It has been said that:

> Young people are invariably trying to solve a problem rather than be one. (Herbert, 1996a)

We can thus see that so many of the effective interventions for young people with other problems are also based on behavioural, skill-orientated and multimodal (packages of care) methods.

Key messages

- Adolescence can be disturbing to young people and parents but most young people come through.
- Young people need to be heard and understood rather than criticised; they are making their own choices.
- Simple cognitive behavioural techniques can resolve anxieties and fears.

Appendices

Websites with useful materials on evidence-based interventions

British Medical Journal. Free on the web in its entirety: www.bmj.com. Many randomised controlled trials in mental health, social care, children and families, prevention etc are published here, also good articles about methods, ethics, dissemination, etc. Bear in mind that only a small proportion of the articles are relevant to social care. However, this still represents a huge bank of high-quality research. Articles are organised into useful collections (see headings such as child psychiatry, adolescents, women's health, psychiatry, evidence-based practice, randomised controlled trials etc).

Center for the Study and Prevention of Violence (CSPV), University of Colorado, produces excellent summaries of research called *Blueprints for Violence Prevention.* They have also done important and innovative research on dissemination of evidence-based interventions: www.colorado.edu/cspv/index.html.

Centre for Evidence-based Social Services, Exeter University. So far a number of useful reviews are available on the website: www.ex.ac.uk/cebss/.

Harvard out-of-school time Program Evaluation Database: www.gse.harvard. edu/hfrp/projects/afterschool/evaldatabase.html.

The Juvenile Justice Clearing House, Prevention Programs, US. Looks at effective juvenile justice programmes: www.fsu.edu/~crimdo/jjclearinghouse

National Clearing House on Child Abuse and Neglect. Includes interesting data: www.nccanch.acf.hhs.gov.

Substance Abuse and Mental Health Services Administration (SAMHSA), US Department of Health and Human Services. Full details of all these programmes and how to implement them can be seen on the SAMHSA website: www.model-programs.samhsa.gov.

York Centre for Reviews and Dissemination. Many useful reviews: www.york.ac.uk/inst/crd/ehcb.htm.

Other UK sites

Social Care Institute for Excellence (SCIE) is undertaking systematic reviews of research studies and current thinking which will be supplemented by fieldwork seminars and interviews to help address gaps in the literature and access emergent knowledge around research use in social care. www.scie.org.uk

UK Centre for Evidence Based Policy and Practice produces systematic reviews and publications around evidence-based policy and practice: www.evidencenetwork. com.

Worldwide web resources for social workers

Center for Intervention & Prevention Research on HIV & Drug Abuse (CIPRHDA). This is an example of information related to research for a specific area of interest: www.columbia.edu/cu/ssw/projects/ciprhda/.

New York University and Mount Sinai School of Medicine in the USA have joined together to provide a search portal for social workers and researchers. Useful as a way into areas of social work intervention and practice as well as some guidance to research evidence: www.nyu.edu/socialwork/wwwrsw/

Useful organisations developing and disseminating evidence-based research

There is much interesting reading material on the following websites:

Campbell Collaboration www.campbellcollaboration.org/

Cochrane Collaboration www.cochrane.org/

Informed Health Online www.informedhealthonline.org/item/aspx

2 Internet resources for parents and young people

Addiction (drugs, alcohol, cigarettes)

Drugscope (UK)
www.drugscope.org.uk
Information on all the types of drugs, their nicknames, their effects and contacts.

National Drugs Helpline (UK)
Freephone: 0800 77 66 00
www.trashed.co.uk
Free advice, counselling and referrals to specialists if you want them to do it for you.

QUIT (UK)
Tel: 0800 002 200
www.quit.org.uk
Free advice on stopping smoking.

Release (UK)
Tel: 020 7729 9904 (Mon–Fri 10am–5pm)
www.release.org.uk
Confidential advice on drug use and issues surrounding the subject.

Adoption/care

Talk Adoption (UK)
Tel: 0808 808 1234 (Tues–Fri 3–9pm)
www.talkadoption.org.uk
Help for those who are adopted.

Who Cares? Trust (UK)
Tel: 0500 564 570
www.thewhocarestrust.org.uk
Advice and information for teenagers who are looked after by local authorities.

Anorexia and bulimia

Eating Disorders Association (UK)
Tel: 0845 634 7650 (youthline) (Mon–Fri 4–6.30pm)
Tel: 0845 634 1414 (adult helpline) (Mon–Fri 8.30am–8.30pm)

www.edauk.com
Advice and support for those with eating disorders.

Bereavement/death

Cruse Bereavement Care (UK)
Tel: 0870 167 1677 (Sun–Wed 3–9pm, Thurs 2–9pm, Fri 2–6pm, Sat 3–6pm)
www.crusebereavementcare.org.uk
Offers counselling for the bereaved.

Especially for young people they have set up **www.rd4u.org.uk**
or Tel: 0808 808 1677.

1000 Deaths
www.1000deaths.com/
Offers support for those who have lost people to suicide.

Bullying

www.bullying.co.uk
Online guide for parents and young people.

ChildLine
Tel: 0800 1111 (or 0800 44 1111 in Scotland) Service available 24 hours a day.

www.childline.org.uk

Contraception/pregnancy

After Abortion (USA)
www.afterabortion.com
A great site for information on abortions and the after effects of them.

Brook Advisory Centre (UK)
Tel: 0800 018 5023
Tel: 020 7617 8000 (24-hour recorded information)
www.brook.org.uk
Advice on contraception.

Family Planning Clinic (UK)
Tel: 020 7837 4044 (Mon–Fri 9am–7pm)
www.fpa.org.uk
Advice on sex issues, and can put you in touch with your nearest clinic.

Domestic violence/abuse

National Domestic Violence Helpline
Tel: 0808 2000 247

General support/advice for young people

ChildLine (UK)
Tel: 0800 1111 (or 0800 44 1111 in Scotland) Service available 24 hours a day
www.childline.org.uk

YOUTH2YOUTH (UK)
Tel: 0208 896 3675 (Mon–Thurs 6.30–9.30pm)

www.youth2youth.co.uk
Support and advice from fully trained 14–23-year-olds.

Mental health

Depression Alliance (UK)
www.depressionalliance.org

MIND mental health charity (UK)
Tel: 08457 660 163 (MINDinfoline (Mon–Fri 9.15am–5.15pm)
Tel: 0845 330 1585 (for deaf or speech impaired; if using BT Textdirect, add 18001)
www.mind.org.uk
Campaigns: **www.mindout.net**

YoungMinds

Tel: 0800 018 2138 (parents' information service)

www.youngminds.org.uk

YoungMinds is the national charity committed to improving the mental health of all children and young people. Provides free, confidential information and advice for any adult with concerns about the mental health of a child or young person and useful leaflets.

Parenting

National Family and Parenting Institute

www.nfpi.org

The National Family and Parenting Institute (NFPI) is an independent charity working to support parents in bringing up their children, to promote the wellbeing of families and to make society more family friendly. Lots of practical information.

Parenting Education and Support Forum

www.parenting-forum.org.uk

The national umbrella body for those who work with parents.

Parentline Plus

Tel: 0808 800 2222 Service available 24 hours a day.

www.parentlineplus.org.uk

Useful information on a range of matters relating to parenting and children.

Rape and sexual abuse

National Society for the Prevention of Cruelty to Children (NSPCC)

Tel: 0808 800 5000

www.nspcc.org.uk

UK charity that provides telephone advice on what to do when you've been abused and support.

For 12–16-year-olds, there is a new confidential advice service from trained advisors.

Rape and Sexual Abuse Support Centre (UK)
Tel: 020 8683 3300 (helpline)
www.rasasc.org.uk (UK)
Offers confidential and non-judgmental help and support to women and girls who have been raped or abused – however long ago.

Safeline (UK)
www.safelinewarwick.co.uk
UK charity for survivors of childhood sexual abuse. Information for friends and relatives, on flashbacks, ritual abuse, panic attacks and more.

Sexual health

BBC sexual health (UK)
www.bbc.co.uk/health/sex/
Offers fact sheets, advice and information on contraception and sexually transmitted infections.

National AIDS helpline (UK)
Tel: 0800 567123
Tel: 0800 371135 (in Urdu)
Tel: 0800 371136 (in Hindi, Wed 6–10pm)
Confidential advice on HIV and AIDS. The call will not show up on a telephone bill.

Sexuality (gay, bisexual, straight)

The Lesbian and Gay Foundation (UK)
Tel: 0161 235 8000 (6–10pm)
www.lgfoundation.org.uk
Merger of Manchester Lesbian and Gay Switchboard and Healthy Gay Manchester.

Stonewall (UK)
Tel: 020 7881 9440
www.stonewall.org.uk
Campaign group working for legal equality and social justice for lesbians, gay men and bisexuals.

Voice of the child

Young Voice
www.young-voice.org
Organisation that elicits and publicises young people's views on a range of issues.

References

See page 4 for an explanation of the star ratings.

Abrahams, C, Mungall, R (1992) *Runaways: exploding the myths. An evaluative report*. NCH/Police Federation, London.

***Achenbach, TM (1991) *Manual for the child behavior checklist 4–18 and 1991 profile*. University of Vermont, Burlington VT.

Advisory Council on the Misuse of Drugs (1993) *Drug education in schools: the need for a new impetus*. The Stationery Office, London.

Albee, GW, Gullotta, T (eds) (1997) *Primary prevention works*. Sage, California Park.

Appleton, PL, Hammond-Rowley, S (2000) Addressing the population burden of child and adolescent mental health problems: a primary care model. *Child and Adolescent Mental Health* 5(1): 9–16.

Appleton, PL, Whitaker, C, Hibbs, R, Hammond-Rowley, S, Wilkinson, C (2002) A population based intervention for psychological problems in young children: a controlled trial. *Spotlight* 98 www.word.wales.gov.uk/content/spotlight/spotlight98-e.pdf.

Aust, R Charp, C, Goulden, C (2002) *Prevalence of drug use: key findings from the 2001/2002 British crime survey*. Home Office Findings 182. Home Office Research, Development and Statistics Directorate, London.

***Barlow, J (1997) *Systematic review of the effectiveness of parent–training programmes in improving behaviour problems in children age 3–10 years*. Oxford Health Services Research Unit, Oxford.

Barnardo's (1995) *All about me board game*. Barnardo's, Barkingside.

Barnardo's Policy, Research and Influencing Unit (1998) *Report for the Social Exclusion Unit*. The Stationery Office, London.

***Barnes, J, Rickman, N (2003) *The early years behaviour checklist handbook*. NFER-Nelson, Windsor.

**Bavolek, SS (1996) *Research and validation report of the nurturing programs: effective family-based approaches to treating and preventing child abuse and neglect.* Family Development Resources Inc, Park City UT.

Besag, V (1989) *Bullies and victims in schools.* Open University Press, Milton Keynes.

Biddulph, S (1998) *Raising boys.* Thorsons, London.

**Birmingham Social Services (1995) *The Wraparound Project final report.* Birmingham Social Services Department, Sparkbrook Area Office, Greencoat House, 261–271 Stratford Road, Birmingham, B11 1QS.

Black, D, Cottrell, D (1993) *Seminars in child and adolescent psychiatry.* Royal College of Psychiatrists, London.

Bone, M, Meltzer, H (1978) *The prevalence of disability among children: OPCS surveys of disability in Great Britain 3.* HMSO, London.

Botvin, GJ, Mihalic, SF, Grotpeter, JK (1998) *Blueprints for violence prevention. Book five: life skills training.* Center for the Study and Prevention of Violence, Boulder, CO (www.colorado.edu).

Bray, JH, Berger, SH (1993) Developmental issues in stepfamilies research project: family relationships and parent-child interactions. *Journal of Family Psychology* 7(1): 76–90.

Bronfenbrenner, U (1979) *The ecology of human development. Experiments in nature and design.* Harvard University Press, Cambridge, MA.

Buchanan, A (1992) *Children who soil: assessment and treatment.* John Wiley and Sons, Chichester.

Buchanan, A (2000) You're walking on eggs. Findings from research into parenting. In Wheal, A (ed) *Working with parents.* Russell House Publishing, Lyme Regis.

Buchanan, A, Wheal, A, Walder, D, Macdonald, S, Coker, R (1993) *Answering back. The view of young people being looked after on the Children Act, 1989.* Department of Social Work Studies, University of Southampton.

**Buchanan, A, Barlow, J, Coucher, M, Hendron, J, Smith, T (1995) *Seen and heard. Families in contact with social services in Wiltshire.* Barnardo's, Barkingside.

***Buchanan, A, Ten Brinke, J-A (1997a) *What happened when they were grown up? Outcomes from parenting experiences*. Joseph Rowntree Foundation, York.

***Buchanan, A and Ten Brinke, J-A (1997b) *Early parenting – adult outcomes*. Joseph Rowntree Foundation, York.

***Buchanan, A, Ten Brinke, J-A (1998) *'Recovery' from emotional and behavioural problems*. Report for NHS Executive Anglia and Oxford.

Buchanan, A, Hunt, J, Bretherton, H, Bream, V (2001) *Families in conflict. Perspectives of children and parents on the Family Court Welfare Service*. Policy Press, Bristol.

Buchanan, A, Flouri, E, Ten Brinke, J-A. (2002) Emotional and behavioural problems in childhood and distress in adult life: risk and protective factors. *Australian and New Zealand Journal of Psychiatry* 36: 521–527.

Buchanan, A, Ritchie, C, Bream, V (2002) *Seen and Heard 2*. Barnardo's, Barkingside.

Buchanan, CM, Maccoby, EE, Dornbusch, SM (1996) *Adolescents after divorce*. Harvard University Press, Cambridge MA.

Calder, MC (1997) *Juveniles and children who sexually abuse: a guide to risk assessment*. Russell House Publishing, Lyme Regis.

**Canny Lads positive images pack. Can be obtained from Longbenton Youth Project, 83a Stoneleigh Avenue, Newcastle upon Tyne NE12 8NT for £12 which includes set of the 4 posters and p&p.

Chesson, R (1999) Bullying: the need for an interagency response *British Medical Journal* 319: 330–331.

Children's Legal Centre (1991) *Mental health handbook*. Children's Legal Centre, London.

Clausen, S (1996) Parenting styles and adolescent drug use behaviours. *Childhood: A Global Journal of Child Research* 3(3): 403–414.

Cohen, D, Richardson, J, Labree, L (1994) Parenting behaviours and the onset of smoking and alcohol use: a longitudinal study. *Paediatrics* 94: 368–375.

Collins, D (1998) *Managing truancy in schools*. Cassell, London.

**Compas, BE (1995) Promoting successful coping during adolescence. In Rutter, M (ed) *Psychosocial disturbances in young people*. Cambridge University Press, Cambridge.

***Cooper, PJ, Murray, L, Hooper, R, West, A (1996) The development and validation of a predictive index for postpartum depression. *Psychological Medicine* 26: 627–634.

***Cooper, PJ, Murray, L (1997) The impact of treatments for postpartum depression on maternal mood and infant development. In Murray, L, Cooper, PJ (eds) *Postpartum depression and child development* (201–220). Guildford, New York.

Craig, WM (1998) The relationship among bullying, victimization, depression, anxiety, and aggression in elementary school children. *Personality and Individual Differences* 24(1): 123–130.

Daniels, H, Visser, J, Cole, T, de Reybekill, N (1998) *Emotional and behavioural difficulties in mainstream school*. Research Report 90. Department for Education and Employment, London.

***Danish, SJ, Meyer, AL, Mash, JM, Howard, CW, Curl, SJ, Brunelle, JP, Owens, S (1998) *Going for the Goal Leader Manual*, Department of Psychology, Virginia Commonwealth University.

**Dearden, S, Aldridge, J, Dearden, S (1998) *Young carers and their families*. Blackwell Science, Oxford.

*De'Ath, E, Slater, D (eds) (1992) *Parenting threads: caring for children when couples part*. Stepfamily Publications, London.

**Deblinger, E, McLeer, SV, Henry, D (1990) Cognitive behavioural treatment for sexually abused children suffering from post-traumatic stress – preliminary findings. *Journal of the American Academy of Child and Adolescent Psychiatry* 29: 747–752.

Department for Education and Employment (1997) *Excellence for all children – meeting special educational needs*. Department for Education and Employment, London.

Department for Education and Employment (1999a) *Handling signs of disaffection in social inclusion: pupil support* . Department for Education and Employment, London.

Department for Education and Employment (1999b) *Making a difference for children and families – Sure Start*. Department for Education and Employment, London.

Department of Health (1995a) *Child protection – messages from research* (1995) HMSO, London.

*Department of Health (1995b) Chief Inspector Letter CI(95)12. Department of Health, London.

Department of Health, Department for Education and Employment and Home Office (1999) *Working together to safeguard children: a guide to inter-agency working to safeguard and promote the welfare of children*. The Stationery Office, London.

Department of Health, Department for Education and Employment and Home Office (2000) *Framework for the assessment of children in need and their families*. Department of Health, London.

Dunn, J, Deater-Deckard, K, Pickering, K, O'Connor, TG, Golding, J (1998) Children's adjustment and prosocial behaviour in step-, single-parent, and non-stepfamily settings: findings from a community study. *Journal of Child Psychology and Psychiatry* 39(8): 1083–1095.

***Durlak, JA (ed) (1997a) *Successful prevention programs for children and adolescents*. Plenum, New York.

***Durlak, JA (ed) (1997b) Prevention of behavioral and social problems. In Durlak, JA, *Successful prevention programs for children and adolescents*. Plenum, New York.

Dyregrov, A (1991) *Grief in children. A handbook for adults*. Jessica Kingsley, London.

D'Zurilla, TJ, Goldfried, MR (1971) Problem solving and behaviour modification. *Journal of Abnormal Psychology* 78: 107–126.

***Eaves, LJ, Silberg, JL, Meyer, JM, Maes, HM, Simonoff, E, Pickles, A, Rutter, M, Neale, MC, Reynolds, CA, Erickson, MT, Heath, AC, Loeber, R, Truett, KR, Hewitt, JK (1997) Genetics and developmental psychopathology: 2 The main effects of genes and environment on behavioural problems in the Virginia twin study of adolescent behavioural development. *Journal of Child Psychology and Psychiatry* 38: 965–980.

Egan, G (1990) *The skilled helper.* Brooks/Cole, Pacific Grove, CA

***Elias, ML, Clabby, JF (1989) *Social decision-making skills: a curriculum guide for the elementary grade.* Aspen Publishers, Rockville, MD.

Elliot, M (1991) *Bullying. A practical guide to coping for schools.* Longman, Harlow.

Espelage, DK, Bosworth, K, Simon, TR (2000) Short-term stability and prospective correlates of bullying in middle-school students: an examination of potential demographic, psychosocial, and environmental influences. *Violence and Victims* 16(4): 411–426.

Evangelou, M, Sylva, K (2001) *Supporting parents as first educators: evaluation from Project PEEP.* www-edstud.ox.ac.uk/research/PEEP%20evaluation%study.doc.

Falkov, A (1998) *Crossing bridges. Training resources for working with mentally ill parents and their children.* Department of Health/ Pavilion Press, Brighton.

***Farrington, D (1979) Longitudinal research on crime and delinquency. In Morris, N, Tonry, M (eds) *Criminal justice: an annual review of research, vol. 2* (289–348). University of Chicago Press, Chicago.

Farrington, D (1996) *Understanding and preventing youth crime.* York Publishing Services, York.

***Fergusson, DM, Lynskey, MT (1996) Adolescent resilience to family adversity. *Journal of Child Psychology and Psychiatry* 9 (4): 483–494.

Fine, MA, Moreland, HR, Schwebel, AI (1983) Long-term effects of divorce on parent-child relationships. *Developmental Psychology* 19(5): 703–713.

Fitzgerald, EM, Mlinarcik, S (2001) The wonders of helping substance exposed children and their parents. *Healing Magazine* 6 www.kidspeace.org/healingmagazine/issue12/pg09.asp.

Fletcher, A, Steinberg, L, Sellers, E (1999) Adolescents' well-being as a function of perceived inter-parental consistency. *Journal of Marriage and the Family* 61 (3) 599–610.

Flouri, E, Buchanan, A (2002a) Childhood predictors of labor force participation in adult life. *Journal of Family and Economic Issues* 23: 101–120.

Flouri, E, Buchanan, A (2002b) Father involvement in childhood and trouble with the police in adolescence: findings from the 1958 British birth cohort. *Journal of Interpersonal Violence* 17: 689–701.

Flouri, E, Buchanan, A (2002c) What predicts good relationships with parents in adolescence and partners in adult life. Findings from the 1958 British birth cohort. *Journal of Family Psychology* 16: 186–198.

Flouri, E, Buchanan, A (2003) The role of father involvement in children's later mental health. *Journal of Adolescence* 26: 63–78.

**Frank, J (1995) *Couldn't care more: a study of young carers and their needs*. Children's Society, London.

Frost, H, Johnson, L, Stein, M, Wallis, L (1997) *Negotiated friendship. Home-Start and the delivery of family support*. Home-Start UK, 2 Salisbury Road, Leicester LE 1 7QR

Garnier, H, Stein, J (2002) An 18 year model of family and peer effects on adolescent drug use and delinquency. *Journal of Youth and Adolescence* 31(1): 45–56.

General Health Questionnaire. Available from www.nfer-nelson.co.uk.

Goldberg, D (1978) *Manual of the general health questionnaire*. NFER-Nelson, Windsor.

Goodman, R (1997a) *Child and adolescent mental health services: reasoned advice to commissioners and providers*. Maudesley Discussion Paper No. 4. Institute of Psychiatry, London.

Goodman, R (1997b) The strengths/difficulties questionnaire. *Journal of Child Psychology and Psychiatry* 38(5): 581–586.

Goodman, R, Scott, S (1997) *Child psychiatry*. Blackwell Science, Oxford.

*Graham P, Hughes, C (1997, reprinted with amendments). *So young, so sad, so listen*. Royal College of Psychiatrists, London.

Grant, T, Ernst, C, McAuliff, S, Streissguth, AP (1997) The difference game: facilitating change in high risk clients. *Families in Society* 78(4): 429–432.

***Grossman, J-B, Tierney, J-P (1998) Does mentoring work? An impact study of the Big Brothers Big Sisters Program. *Evaluation Review* 22(3): 403–426.

Hardman, E, Joughin, C (1998) *Focus on clinical audit in child and adolescent mental health services*. Royal College of Psychiatrists, London.

***Harrington, R, Wood, S, Verdyn, C (1998) Clinically depressed adolescents. In Graham, P (ed) *Cognitive behaviour therapy for children and families*. Cambridge University Press, Cambridge.

Hawton, K (1986) *Suicide and attempted suicide among children and adolescents*. Sage, London.

Haynie, DL, Nansel, T, Eitel, P, Crump, AD, Saylor, K, Yu, K, Simons-Morton, B (2001) Bullies, victims, and bully/victims: distinct groups of at-risk youth. *Journal of Early Adolescence* 21(1): 29–49.

**Health Advisory Service (1994) *Suicide prevention – the challenge confronted*. HMSO, London.

Health Advisory Service (1995) *Child and mental health services: together we stand*. HMSO, London.

***Henggeler, SW, Mihalic, SF, Rone, L, Thomas, C, Timmons-Mitchell, J (1998) *Blueprints for violence prevention: multisystemic therapy*. Blue Print Publications, Boulder CO.

**Herbert, M (1996a) *Banishing bad behaviour* (PACTS). British Psychological Society, Leicester.

Herbert, M (1996b) *Post-traumatic stress disorder in children*. (PACTS). British Psychological Society, Leicester.

**Hester, M, Radford, L (1996) *Domestic violence and child contact arrangements in England and Denmark*. Policy Press, Bristol.

**Hester, M, Kelly, L, Radford, J (eds) (1996) *Women, violence and male power*. Open University Press, Milton Keynes.

Home Office (1998) *Supporting families – a consultation document*. Home Office, London.

Home Office (2000a) *Parenting policy forum*. Home Office, London.

Home Office (2000b) *Domestic violence: break the chain. Multi-agency guidance for addressing domestic violence*. Home Office, London. www.homeoffice.gov.uk/docs/mag.htm.

Hylton, C (1995) *Coping with change: family transitions in multi-cultural communities*. Stepfamily Publications, London.

Iwaniec, D (1995) *The emotionally abused and neglected child: identification, assessment, intervention*. John Wiley and Sons, Chichester.

Jaffee, SR, Moffitt, TE Caspir, A, Taylor, A (2003) Life with (or without) father: the benefits of living with two biological parents depend on the father's antisocial behaviour. *Child Development* 74(1): 109–126.

**Kane, B (1979) Children's concepts of death. *Journal of Genetic Psychology* 134: 141–145.

**Katz, A, Buchanan, A, Ten Brinke, J-A (1998) *The can do girls*. The Body Shop, obtainable from Department of Applied Social Studies and Research, University of Oxford.

**Katz, A, Buchanan, A, McCoy, A (1999) *Leading lads* (1999) Arcadia/Young Minds/University of Oxford. Obtainable from *Young Minds*, 12 Bridge Gardens, East Molesley, Surrey KT8 9HU.

Katz, A, Buchanan, A, Bream, V (2000) *Bullying in Britain – testimonies from teenagers*. Young Voice, London.

***Kendall, PC, Flannery-Schroeder, E, Panichelli-Mindel, SM, Southam-Gerow, M (1997) Therapy for youth with anxiety disorders: a second randomized clinical trial. *Journal of Consulting Clinical Psychology* 65: 366–380.

***Kitzman, H, Olds, DL, Henderson, CR, Hanks, C, Cole, R, Tatelbaum, R, McConnochie, KM, Sidora, K, Luckey, DW, Shaver, D, Englhardt, K, James, D,

Barnard, K (1997) Effect of prenatal and infancy home visitation by nurses on pregnancy outcomes, childhood injuries and repeated childbearing. A randomized controlled trial. *Journal of the American Medical Association* 278: 644–652.

Kovacs, M, Devlin, B (1998) Internalizing disorders in childhood. *Journal of Child Psychology and Psychiatry* 39(1): 47–63.

Kumpfer, KL (1987) *Prevention services for children of substance abusing adults.* National Institute of Drug Abuse: Final Technical Report. R18DA 02758-101/02 and DA 03888-01. NIDA, Rockville MD.

Lamborn, SD, Mounts, NS, Steinberg, L, Dornbusch, SM (1991) Patterns of competence and adjustment among adolescents from authoritative, authoritarian, indulgent, and neglectful families. *Child Development* 62(5): 1049–1065.

Laming, H (2003) *The Victoria Climbie inquiry: report.* The Stationery Office, London.

Lipsey, M (1995) What do we learn from 400 studies on the effectiveness of treatment with juvenile delinquents? In McGuire, J (ed) *What works: reducing reoffending.* John Wiley and Sons, Chichester.

LoSciuto, L, Rajala, A, Townsend, TN, Taylor, AS (1996) An outcome evaluation of Across Ages: An intergenerational mentoring approach to drug prevention. *Journal of Adolescent Research* 11: 116–129.

***McCann, J, James, A, Wilson, S, Dunn, G (1996) Prevalence of psychiatric disorders in young people in the care system. *British Medical Journal* 313: 1529–1530.

McClun, LA, Merrell K (1998) Relationship of perceived parenting styles, locus of control orientation, and self-concept among junior high age students. *Psychology in the Schools* 35(4): 381–390.

***McCord, J (1992) The Cambridge-Somerville study: a pioneering longitudinal experimental study of delinquency prevention. In McCord, J, Tremblay, RE, *Preventing antisocial behavior: interventions from birth through adolescence.* Guildford Press, New York.

***McKey, HR, Condelli, L, Ganson, H, Barrett, B, McConkey, C, Platz, M (1985) *The impact of Head Start on children, families and communities: final report of the Head*

Start evaluation, synthesis and utilisation project. The Head Start Bureau, Administration for Children and Youth and Families, Office of Human Development Services, US Department of Health and Human Services, Washington, DC.

Marsh, P, Crow, G (1998) *Family group conferences in child welfare.* Blackwells, Oxford.

Meltzer, H, Gatward, R, Goodman, R, Ford, T (2000) *The mental health of children and adolescents in Great Britain.* The Stationery Office, London.

Mental Health Foundation (1999)*The big picture: promoting children and young people's mental health.* Mental Health Foundation, London.

Miller, WR, Rollnick, S (2002) *Motivational interviewing.* 2nd edn. Guildford Press, New York.

Ministerial Group on the Family (1998) *Supporting families: a consultation document.* The Stationery Office, London.

Morgan, R (1981) *Childhood incontinence.* Heinemann Medical Books, London.

Mynard, H, Joseph, S (1997) Bully/victim problems and their association with Eysenck's personality dimensions in 8 to 13 year olds. *British Journal of Educational Psychology* 67: 51–54.

Narramore, B, Lewis, VC (1990) *Parenting teens: a road map through the ages and stages of adolescence.* Tyndale House, Carol Stream IL.

National Family and Parenting Institute (2001a) *Listening to parents, their worries, their solutions.* NFPI, London.

National Family and Parenting Institute (2001b) *National mapping of family services in England and Wales.* NFPI, London.

Noble, M, Smith, T (1994) 'Children in need': using geographical information systems to inform strategic planning for social service provision. *Children and Society* 8(4): 360–376.

Noble, M, Wright, G, Dibben, C, Smith, GAN, McLennan, D, Anttila, C, Barnes, H, Mokhtar, C, Noble, S, Avenell, D, Gardner, J, Covizzi, I, Lloyd, M (2004) *The English indices of deprivation 2004.* ODPM Publications, Wetherby.

***Novaco, RW (1975) *Anger control: the development and evaluation of an experimental treatment.* DC Heath, Lexington, MA.

Oakley, A (1992) Social support in pregnancy: methodology and findings of a 1-year follow-up study. *Journal of Reproductive and Infant Psychology* 10: 219–231.

***Oakley, A, Rajan, L, Grant, A (1990) Social support and pregnancy outcome. *British Journal of Obstetrics and Gynaecology* 97: 155–162.

***Olds, DL, Eckenrode, J, Henderson, CR, Kitzman, H, Powers, J, Cole, R, Sidord, K, Morris, P, Pettitt, LM, Luckley, D (1997) Long term effects of home visitation on maternal life course and child abuse and neglect. Fifteen-year follow-up of a randomized trial. *Journal of the American Medical Association* 278: 637–643.

***Olweus, D (1993) *Bullying in school: what we know and what we can do.* Blackwell, Oxford.

Pagani, L, Boulerice, B, Tremblay, RE, Vitaro, F (1997) Behavioural development in children of divorce and remarriage. *Journal of Child Psychology and Psychiatry* 38(7): 769–781.

***Patterson, G, Narrett, G (1990) The development of a reliable and valid treatment programme for aggressive young children. *International Journal of Mental Health* 19(3): 19–26.

***Pedro-Caroll, JL, Cowen, EL (1985) The children of divorce intervention program. An investigation of the efficacy of a school-based prevention programme. *Journal of Consulting and Clinical Psychology* 14: 277–290.

PEEP Annual Report 1997–1998. The PEEP Centre, Peers School, Sandy Lane West, Littlemore, Oxford OX4 5JZ.

Perry, DG, Kusel, SJ, Perry, LC (1988) Victims of peer aggression. *Developmental Psychology* 24(6): 807–814.

***Pfannenstiel J, Seltzer, D (1985) *New parents as teachers project: evaluation report.* Research and Training Associates, Overland Park KS.

Plomin, R (1994) Genetic research and identification of environmental influences. The Emmanual Miller Memorial Lecture, 1993. *Journal of Child Psychology and Psychiatry* 35(5): 817–835.

Plomin, R (2001) Genetics and behaviour. *The Psychologist* 14(3): 134–153.

***Prochasta, JO, DiClementi, CC (1982) Trans-theoretical therapy: toward a more integrated model of change. *Psychotherapy: Theory, Research and Practice* 19: 276–288.

Pudney, S (2002) *The road to ruin? Sequences of initiation into drug use and offending by young people in Britain.* Home Office Research Study 253. Home Office Research, Development and Statistics Directorate, London.

**Richardson, AJ (1998) *Fathers plus: an audit of work with fathers throughout the north east of England.* Children North-East, 1a Claremont Street, Newcastle-upon-Tyne, NE 2 4 AH, Tel: 0191 232 3741. Fax: 0191 221 0451.

Robins, LE (1992) The role of prevention experiments in discovering causes of children's antisocial behaviour. In McCord, J, Tremblay, RE, *Preventing antisocial behaviour.* Guildford Press, New York.

***Rodgers, B, Pryor, J (1998) *Divorce and separation: the outcomes for children.* Joseph Rowntree Foundation, York.

Roland, E, Munthe, E (eds) (1989) *Bullying, an international perspective.* David Fulton Publishers, London.

***Ronan, T (1998) Linking developmental and emotional elements into child and family cognitive-behavioural therapy. In Graham, P (ed) *Cognitive-behaviour therapy for children and families* pp 1–17. Cambridge University Press, Cambridge.

Rose, S, Bisson, J, Wessley, S (2001) Psychological debriefing for preventing post traumatic stress disorder (PTSD) (Cochrane Review). In *The Cochrane Library* issue 2, 2004. John Wiley, Chichester.

Royal College of Psychiatrists (1982) The management of parasuicide in young people under 16: report from the Child and Adolescent Section. *Bulletin of the Royal College of Psychiatrists* 182–185.

Rutter, M, Cox, M, Tupling, G, Berger, M, Yule, N (1975) Attainment and adjustment in two geographical areas. Prevalence of psychiatric disorder. *Journal of Child Psychology and Psychiatry* 22(4): 375–395.

***Rutter, M, Giller, H, Hagell, A (1998) *Antisocial behavior by young people.* Cambridge University Press, New York.

Rutter, M (1975) *Helping troubled children.* Penguin, Harmondsworth.

Rutter, M, Tizard, J, Whitmore, K (eds) (1970) *Education, health and behaviour.* Longman, London.

***Rutter, M, Quinton, D (1984) Long-term follow-up of women institutionalised in childhood. Factors promoting good function in adult life. *British Journal of Developmental Psychology* 2: 191–204.

***Rutter, M, Smith, D (eds) (1995) *Psychosocial disorders in young people.* John Wiley and Sons, Chichester.

Rutter, M, Tizard, J, Whitmore, K (eds) (1970) *Education, health and behaviour.* Longman, London.

***Schweinhart, I, Weikart, D (1993) *A summary of significant benefits: the High/Scope Perry Pre-School study through age 27.* High/Scope Press, Ypsilanti.

Slee, PT, Rigby, K (1993) Australian school children's self appraisal of interpersonal relations: The bullying experience. *Child Psychiatry and Human-Development* 23(4): 273–282.

**Smith, C (1998) *Parenting programmes.* National Children's Bureau, London.

**Smith, T (1998) Parents and the community: parents' views and mapping need. In Buchanan, A, Hudson, BL (eds) *Parenting, schooling and children's behaviour.* Ashgate, Aldershot.

Social Exclusion Unit (1998) *Truancy and school exclusion report.* Cmnd. 3957. The Stationery Office, London.

Social Exclusion Unit (2002) *Young Runaways.* The Stationery Office, London.

***Spivack, G, Platt, JA, Shure, M (1976) *The problem-solving approach to adjustment.* Jossey-Bass, San Francisco CA.

Steinberg, L (2000) The family at adolescence: transition and transformation. *Journal of Adolescent Health* 27(3): 170–178.

Steinberg, L, Steinberg, W (1994) *Crossing paths: how your child's adolescence triggers your own crisis.* Simon and Schuster, New York.

Sutton, A (1996) *Report prepared for the Child and Adolescent Executive sub-committee of the Royal College of Psychiatrists.* Royal College of Psychiatrists, London.

Sweeting, H, West, P (1995) Family life and health in adolescence. A role for culture in the health inequalities debate? *Social Science and Medicine* 40(2): 163–175.

Sylva, K (1998) *Seminar to the Centre for Research into Parenting and Children, University of Oxford, November 1998*

***Sylva, K, Colman, P (1998) Pre-school interventions to prevent behaviour problems and school failure. In Buchanan, A, Hudson, BL (eds) *Parenting, schooling and children's behaviour.* Ashgate, Aldershot.

Sylva K, Sammons, P, Melhuish, EC, Siraj-Blatchford, I, Taggart, B (1999) *The effective provision of pre-school education (EPPE) project: technical paper 1 – an introduction of EPPE.* DfEE/Institute of Education, University of London, London.

***Szapocznik, J, Hervis, OE (2001) Brief Strategic Family Therapy (BSFT): a revised manual. In *National Institute on Drug Abuse Treatment Manual.* NIDA, Rockville MD.

***Taylor, AS, Bressler, J (2000) *Mentoring across generations: partnerships for positive youth development.* Klewer Academic Board/Plenum Press, New York.

Utting, D (1998*) Suggestions for the UK: an overview of possible action.* Paper presented at 'Cross Departmental Review on Provision for Young Children' hosted by Joseph Rowntree Foundation, Institution of Civil Engineers, London, 11 March.

**Vernon, J, Sinclair, R (1998) *Maintaining children in school. The contribution of social services departments.* National Children's Bureau, London.

Vuchinich, S, Hetherington, EM, Vuchinich, RA, Clingemeel, WG (1991) Parent-child interaction and gender differences in early adolescents' adaptation to stepfamilies. *Developmental Psychology* 27(4): 618–626.

Ward, H (1995) *Looking after children. Research into practice. The second report to the Department of Health on assessing outcomes in childcare.* HMSO, London.

Watson, D (ed) (1985) *A code of ethics for social work.* Routledge and Kegan Paul, London.

**Webster A, Buchanan, A (1982) Bedtime without battles. *British Journal of Social Work* 12: 197–204.

***Webster-Stratton, C (1992) *The incredible years – a trouble-shooting guide for parents of children age 3–8.* Umbrella Press, Toronto.

***Webster-Stratton, C (1998) Adopting and implementing empirically supported interventions. In Buchanan, A, Hudson, BL (eds) *Parenting, schooling and children's behaviour.* Ashgate, Aldershot.

***Webster-Stratton, C, Hammond, M (1997) Treating children with early onset conduct problems: a comparison of child and parent training interventions. *Journal of Consulting Clinical Psychology* 65: 93–109.

***Webster-Stratton, C, Hancock, L (1998) Training for parents of young children with conduct problems: content, methods and therapeutic processes. In Briesmeister, J, Schaefer, E (eds) *Handbook of parent training.* John Wiley and Sons, New York.

Weiss, RS (1984) The impact of marital dissolution on income and consumption in single-parents households. *Journal of Marriage and the Family* 46: 115–126.

Welsh, E, Buchanan, A, Flouri, E, Lewis, J (forthcoming July 2004) 'Involved' fathering and child well-being: fathers' involvement with secondary school age children. National Children's Bureau, London, with Joseph Rowntree Foundation, York.

Westman, JC (1983) The impact of divorce on teenagers. *Clinical Pediatrics* 22(10): 692–697.

Wheal, A (ed) (1995) *The foster carers' handbook.* Russell House Publishing, Lyme Regis.

Wheal, A, Buchanan, A (1994, reprinted 1999) *Answers for carers: you and young people in your care.* Pavilion, Brighton.

Whitehouse, E, Pudney, W (1996) *Volcano in my tummy*. New Society Publishers, Gabriola Island BC .

***Winter, MM, McDonald, DS (1997) Parents as teachers: investing in good beginnings for children. In Albee, GW, Gullotta, TP (eds) *Primary prevention works*. Sage, California Park.

***Wood, AJ, Harrington, RC, Moore, A (1996) Controlled trial of a brief cognitive-behavioural intervention in adolescent patients with depressive disorders. *Journal of Child Psychology and Psychiatry* 37: 737–746.

**Yule, W, Udwin, O, Murdoch, K (1990) The 'Jupiter' sinking: effects on children's fears, depression and anxiety. *Journal of Child Psychology and Psychiatry* 31: 1051–1061.

Index